SMALL
BUSINESS
BIG
LIFE

SMALL BUSINESS
BIG
LIFE

FIVE STEPS TO CREATING A GREAT LIFE WITH YOUR OWN SMALL BUSINESS

LOUIS BARAJAS

THOMAS NELSON
Since 1798

NASHVILLE   DALLAS   MEXICO CITY   RIO DE JANEIRO   BEIJING

"The Paradoxical Commandments" from Anyway: The Paradoxical Commandments by Kent M. Keith, copyright © 2001 by Kent M. Keith. Used in North America by permission of G.P. Putnam's Sons, a division of Penguin Group (USA) Inc. Used in the United Kingdom and in Spanish by permission of Inner Ocean Publishing.

FASTSIGNS is a registered trademark of FASTSIGNS International, Inc.

Published in Nashville, Tennessee by Thomas Nelson. Thomas Nelson is a trademark of Thomas Nelson, Inc.

Thomas Nelson, Inc., titles may be purchased in bulk for educational, business, fund-raising, or sales promotional use. For information, please e-mail SpecialMarkets@ThomasNelson.com.

Library of Congress Cataloging-in-Publication Data
Barajas, Louis, 1961-
    Small business, big life / Louis Barajas.
      p. cm.
    ISBN-13: 978-1-4016-0336-6 (hardcover)
    ISBN-10: 1-4016-0336-X (hardcover)
    ISBN-13: 978-1-59555-128-3 (trade paper)
    ISBN-10: 1-59555-128-X (trade paper)
    1. Small business. 2. Small business—Management. 3. Success. 4. Success in business. I. Title.
    HD2341.B268 2007
    658.02'2—dc22
                                                          2007001070

Printed in the United States of America
07 08 09 10 11 CHG 6 5 4 3 2 1

This book is dedicated to my father.

When I was young, I never fully appreciated how you were always there for me. I fondly remember that you always took the time to help me shoot hoops or play catch, no matter how busy your life was. As a child, I marveled at your speed as a soccer player. Unfortunately, I never inherited your speed, but I did inherit your entrepreneurial gene. As a teenager, never did I realize that, when I helped you with your start-up company, I would be getting some of the best business experience of my life. I appreciate the opportunity to have worked with you and learned the virtues of hard work and integrity that you taught me. I also learned from you that anyone in America has the opportunity to fulfill the American Dream when they have enough desire and the willingness to work hard.

As a man, I now appreciate your enthusiasm for enjoying life to the fullest and giving me the courage to go after my dreams. I will never take for granted how you took care of our family no matter how hard it got financially or how many obstacles you had to overcome. We always had food on the table and love in our home. Thank you for being my role model and showing me how to take care of my family.

Finally, I admire how much you have always loved my mother. Your example led me to attract the woman of my dreams and understand completely that all we can leave on this earth are memories with our loved ones. Angie and I are better partners and better parents because of you.

I love you—Your Son

Contents

CONTENTS

Acknowledgments

Writing the acknowledgment section is very difficult for me. I am always worried that I may unintentionally forget someone. There are people in my life who have been great mentors and contributors to my writing and consulting—way too many to mention—but they all have been authors. Some of the authors I have met, and some I will never get the chance to meet. They all have been a major influence in my life. I always wondered if what they wrote would apply to immigrants or to the poor. I have used my wealth and business planning firm as a test kitchen to try out their wise business, finance, and self-improvement recipes with our clients and have taught these same principles in seminars and workshops in underserved communities throughout the nation. With some added cultural spices that I have thrown in, I have made most of their recipes work. To all these authors (some of whose names you'll find in appendix D), thank you for all your wisdom.

Without the help of my business team, I could never have the opportunity to touch so many people. I want to especially thank Aaron Muñoz and Gilbert Cerda. You two gentlemen are the backbone of our company. Your unselfish attitude, dedication, and hard work have helped build a financial planning and business consulting firm founded on the highest degree of love and integrity. I also wish to thank David Bach. David has been a good friend, mentor, and inspiration to me. David, you are a man who will continually be blessed many times over because of the size of your heart and your dedication to help the masses.

Victoria St. George of Just Write has been a huge blessing in my life. Vicki takes my writing to another level. She knows what my soul is trying to write even when I have a hard time coming up with the right words. Vicki, I want you to know that I marvel at the ease with which words flow from you. This is our second project together, and I know that there will be even bigger projects to work on together in the future.

I still can't believe that Shannon Miser-Marvin, my agent at Dupree Miller, represents me. Her list of clients is a Who's Who of famous authors. I feel privileged and honored that you are willing to represent an author who writes for the underserved. Thank you for believing in my dream to transform underrepresented communities and to help them achieve greater abundance.

My publisher, Thomas Nelson, has been also an absolute gift. From day one the staff there believed in me and my message. My editor, Larry Stone, has been unfailingly helpful with his guidance on how to make this book better and more reader-friendly. The encouragement and support I've received from Thomas Nelson have made it possible for this book to be available to people all over the world.

Above all, I want to thank my family. There is nothing more important than family. Mom, your courage and grace in handling your health challenges have been inspiring to me. You continue to be my rock. I can always count on you for unconditional love and support. I also have incredibly supportive in-laws. I have two daughters who don't have a clue as to what I do, but who love me no matter what. My third kid is Eddie, not really a kid anymore. Eddie has been put in the same position that my dad put me in many years ago. When I knew my dad needed help, I stepped up to the plate to do what was needed. Eddie, I want you to know that you have done the same for me. You continually surprise me with your care for people in need.

Angie is the love of my life, my best friend, confidante, and business travel companion. Angie is devoted to our children, our marriage, and my cause to bring wealth and business wisdom to the poor and underserved communities. When I am exhausted and feel like giving up, she encourages me and reminds me of the love and diligence that are needed if we are to help to transform our communities. I thank God for her every day.

Finally, I want to thank all the readers who have sent me letters and e-mails telling me how much their lives have been changed with my previous book, *The Latino Journey to Financial Greatness*. Writing a book and going on the road to take my message to the masses can sometimes be overwhelming. Your heartfelt responses give me the courage to continue my life's work.

Foreword

by Joel Ewanick

At Hyundai we are proud to encourage good thinking. We believe that celebrating good thinking is based on three pillars. The first pillar is discovery. We define discovery as exposing unexamined assumptions in entertaining and educational ways. The second pillar is better living. We feel that better living is about delivering tips and insights that make life easier, more productive and more rewarding. Finally, our third pillar is a better world. We want to make the world a better place by implementing and associating with programs that benefit the communities in which we live and do business.

For almost two decades, Louis Barajas has been a national role model for helping underserved communities focus on personal finances and entrepreneurship through innovative, inspiring, and impactful tools. We believe that Louis Barajas' books, speeches, and workshops represent a combination of all Hyundai's three pillars. That is why we are proud to sponsor the Small Business, Big Life book tour. By making this book complimentary to you, we know that Hyundai is impacting people all over America for the greater good, by providing them a guide to live a better, richer, and more purposeful life.

I hope that you enjoy this book as much as we have.

Joel Ewanick
Vice President, Marketing
Hyundai Motor America

HYUNDAI

HyundaiUSA.com

Introduction

My father, Agapito Barajas, was thirty-seven years old and had been in this country for nineteen years when he started his small business. Like millions of people from all over the world, he had immigrated to the United States because he wanted a better life for himself and his family. Both my parents had moved to Los Angeles from Mexico. They met here, got married very young, and had two children, a boy and a girl, in short order. My brother was born almost eleven years later.

My parents raised us in the barrio of East Los Angeles. My father, who came from a city near Guadalajara, Mexico, never graduated from high school. He worked long hours in a lighting manufacturing plant to support our family and took extra jobs on the side to make ends meet. But he quickly realized that the most he could ever make at the lighting company was a dollar or two above minimum wage, so he started his own ornamental iron contracting business.

Where I grew up, my family didn't know any CPAs, business consultants, or financial planners. My father had to rely on his eleven-year-old son, me, to help him—not just to clean up around the shop but also to assist with many other aspects of the business. Since I was the only one in the family who spoke fluent English, I had to be my dad's translator. I would go with him to see a new client and give the client the estimate: "My father says it's going to cost this much." Then I would translate the reply: "Hey, Dad, they're saying this and this." My dad would come back and say, "No, tell them that it's going to be this much."

Often I would put my own spin on the answer: "My dad says the job's going to cost this, but he can throw in X and Y." Then I would tell my dad, "If you do this, you'll get the job." A Japanese client and a Mexican contractor would then shake hands, without ever speaking to each other directly. The client would give my dad a deposit, get a little handwritten receipt in return, and my dad would come in and put wrought iron doors or window guards on the house.

By the time I was thirteen, I was doing my dad's taxes and bookkeeping. I saw small business at its most demanding—the unending hours, the difficulties finding jobs, the financial burden a start-up business can place on a family. I remember clearly that the year my dad started his business, my mom bought him an inexpensive coat for the colder weather. Like a windbreaker, the coat was covered with plasticlike waterproof material. One day while working with a welding torch, my dad burned a big patch of plastic off the outside of the coat. But he wore that coat for four more years—that's how long it took my parents to be able to afford to buy him a new one.

My father worked hard and treated his clients and employees with respect and integrity. He faced many obstacles over the years, and he had to have the heart and the courage of a lion to survive. Sometimes I wonder how we ever made it. But we did. My dad stayed in business for thirty-three years and provided for his family the best way he knew how. Meanwhile, I graduated from high school and attended UCLA on scholarship. I earned my MBA from Claremont Graduate School, became a Certified Financial Planner, and was hired by one of the top accounting firms in Orange County. I had a house in Irvine and a Lexus; I'd married a great woman, and we had two beautiful daughters. I had it made.

At the same time, I watched my dad still going out six, even seven days a week, putting far too many hours into his wrought iron business. After the first few, difficult years, it was a good living for himself and his family. But while Dad was always able to play catch with me and go to my basketball games when I was young, my brother (who's eleven years younger) had a completely different experience. Once my dad started his business, he was rarely home in time to go to my brother's baseball games or school conferences. Dad spent all his afternoons and evenings trying to build his business so his family would have some small amount of financial security. He was getting older and older, and he was still digging ditches and bending iron and installing incredibly heavy gates, doors, and security bars.

At sixty-nine years of age, after thirty-three years of working with ornamental iron, my dad decided to retire. But when he went to sell his business, he couldn't find anyone to buy it. *He* was the business's main asset—his ability to work the iron and, more important, to gain his customers' trust. Without him, the only real value of the business was in the stock and the storefront.

Dad tried to sell the business to his three employees, but they didn't even have enough money for a down payment. So after thirty-three years, my dad transferred ownership of the business to Ricardo, the employee who'd been with him the longest. Luckily, Dad had been smart enough to invest in a few pieces of real estate over the years; otherwise, his retirement nest egg would be small indeed. Today his only sources of income are the rents from his properties.

It was to help people like my dad that I decided to leave my comfortable job and life in Orange County to open a financial and business planning firm in the East Los Angeles barrio where I grew up. And I ran into some of the same obstacles my dad did—the obstacles that almost every entrepreneur faces. It was months before I saw any income at all. I worked seven days a week. I put up flyers, did free talks for groups, networked like mad. I did everything I could to convince people to use me to prepare their tax returns and help them plan for a more secure financial future.

It wasn't easy; most of the people in East Los Angeles never even considered financial or business planning. I had been earning a great income at my old company, but my first year on my own I made less than $12,000. But over the months more and more clients came to me to prepare their taxes, and I showed them how to create a more secure future for themselves and their children. My client roster became large enough that I added an administrative assistant, then another tax preparer, and then a partner. My business grew and prospered.

Over the years, I noticed that many of my clients either had their own businesses or wanted to start one. Most of them were like my dad: They had been working in dead-end jobs, and the only way they could see to make more money was to start a business. But often they ended up in what I call the *self-employment trap.* They were working for themselves, but if they left the business to take a day off, they didn't make a cent of income. What they had wasn't a business; it was a job, one in which they had to work much harder than they had ever worked for any other company.

I know the toll a small business can take on the life of an entrepreneur because I, too, have paid the price. In those first years of getting my business started, I remember coming home late at night and having my dog growl at me as if I were a prowler. My own dog didn't recognize me! The first few years of my daughters' lives I wasn't around as much as I wanted to be, because my other "baby"—the business—demanded almost all of my time and energy. And my wife felt as if she were at the bottom of the ladder when it came to my attention. We grew apart and eventually divorced.

I was lucky and smart—and I learned my lesson. I didn't want to end my life not having *lived* my life. So I read books and studied the strategies of some of the top business thinkers of our time. I devoured Michael Gerber's *E-Myth* books, Dan Sullivan's *How the Best Get Better,* Jim Collins' *Good to Great,* John C. Maxwell's *The 21 Irrefutable Laws of Leadership,* and Marcus Buckingham's *Now, Discover Your Strengths.* I combined some of their concepts with my years of experience coaching and helping small business owners. I tested my ideas in my own business and then with the clients of our firm.

I discovered that when people built their life foundation first, they stood a much better chance of building successful small businesses. And when our clients created what we called their *life blueprint,* which made business one of their priorities but not the only priority, and they followed the other steps of building their business, they could be successful entrepreneurs and have loving, close relationships at the same time.

Through the years, I've taken my own advice. Today I have a great business that focuses on helping entrepreneurs create successful businesses, secure financial futures for themselves and their families, and happy, fulfilling lives. I've married a wonderful woman, Angie, and she and her son, Eddie, work in my company. I spend time both *in* my business and *on* my business. I'm recognized nationally as a personal finance and small business expert. I travel the country speaking to groups, and I have consulted online for people all over the world as AOL's Latino small business expert. I love what I do, the people I'm around, and what I'm building for my family's future.

I tell you this not to impress you, but because I believe *every entrepreneur can have a business and earn more for their families while still having a fulfilling life.* You, too, can create a business that will flourish while it gives you more time, money, freedom, and satisfaction. In this book I will share with you some of the same recommendations that we make to our clients. I know that these lessons work because we have taught this material for over sixteen years and have seen its principles transform businesses and lives.

We also use these lessons each and every day in my own company. Like you, I'm a small business owner with customers, employees, and growth opportunities (we like to call our problems "opportunities"). I know and feel your pain—the occasionally excruciating pain—of running a small business. I have spent the last sixteen years coming up with solutions for your "opportunities." I want to share with you ways to start, build, and run a successful small business and still spend time with your family. You'll learn how to discover what's truly important to you in your life so that you can create a business that adds joy to your life rather than draining your time and energy.

Small Business, Big Life is not for the next Bill Gates or a hotshot MBA on the fast track. Instead, it's for the rest of us—ordinary folks who have more dreams than education, capital, or resources; hardworking souls who want a better life for their families; single parents whose jobs are in jeopardy because they have had to miss some work when the kids are sick; the kind of big-dreaming individuals who have made this country great for more than two hundred years. Our businesses are too small to use big consulting companies like Accenture or KPMG. Most of us aren't ready for the detailed approach of consulting programs that require a minimum three-year time commitment and thousands of dollars. We aren't familiar with the services offered by the Small Business Administration (SBA), Service Corps of Retired Executives (SCORE), and other programs. But we need the help, probably more than anyone, because we are so small. We've invested our time, savings, and love—our lives—to build something that will make our families more prosperous. We deserve the best help available.

My goal is to make sure you get the greatest return on your investment in this book. I believe that you hold in your hands a valuable guide that can help you take the spark of desire for a better life for your family and turn it into the warm fire of a successful small business, one that will provide the lasting legacy of economic and personal freedom, happiness, and fulfillment that are the true definition of success. I look forward to hearing your stories as you walk the path to creating a small business, big life!

1

Why Start a Business?

Two aspects of the American dream are ingrained in the minds of most people in this country. The first is to own your own home. The second—and I believe more powerful—is to create and own a successful business. Small business is the foundation of the United States economy and the bedrock of its prosperity.

As one of AOL's Latino "Mi Negocio" small business experts, with my own small business (a financial and business planning company), many of my clients are immigrants, minorities, and the working poor. These are men and women just like my father, who came to this country with limited education and no training in any skill. After nineteen years with a lighting manufacturing company, my father left his job because he wanted more for himself and his family. Like hundreds of thousands of people every year, he thought to himself, *I can do better on my own*, and he started his own wrought iron business. He worked very hard, treated his customers fairly, and supported his family with the income from his business for thirty-three years.

Almost every workday I get calls and e-mails from people and meet with clients who, like my dad, either want to have or already own some kind of business. I've seen their success stories and failures. I've seen people who are just in the dreaming phase and those who are ready to cash out and sell their thriving enterprises. I've lived the ups and downs of starting and running two small businesses myself. And I've observed that far too many people have little idea of why they want to create a business, much less how to run one.

According to many business surveys, the three most common reasons to start a business are:

- to make more money

- to have more control of your time

- to sell a better product or deliver a better service

In my experience, however, there is another, more compelling reason why people decide to start their own businesses: they're forced into it by economic necessity. No matter what they do, they can't earn enough to support themselves and their families on their current income, and they believe a small business is the answer to their situation.

Henry David Thoreau once wrote, "The mass of men live lives of quiet desperation." Every single day I see people who are living lives of quiet *financial* desperation. If you ask how things are going, they'll smile and say, "Fine," never telling you they just went home and had a fight with their spouse, who spent an extra forty dollars that week to replace a pair of shoes. Or they're always looking to spend as little as possible for anything. Recently a friend of mine bought tires for twenty dollars each. "Isn't it great to find tires for so little?" she said to me. The tires weren't new, of course; they were retreads. But she couldn't afford anything better.

Financial desperation isn't confined to people who live in rundown neighborhoods. Recently, I heard a morning DJ on one of the radio stations here in Los Angeles talk about being part of the "squeezed" middle class. He said, "If someone makes over $100,000, they're supposed to be in the top ten percent of all wage earners in this country. But if you fall into that category, please call me and tell me if you feel rich. I live in L.A. and I make six figures, but between the house payment, insurance, taxes, car expenses, and just living, I'm barely squeaking by. When I or my wife or my kids need new shoes, we don't go to Nordstrom, we go to Payless. The other day I went to Taco Bell, and I had to look through my car to find enough spare change to buy a couple of tacos. Anybody else out there in the same boat?" For the next hour, the guy couldn't take the calls fast enough. In today's modern world it seems that earning enough to pay for the basics of living is getting harder and harder.

Most people I know do not want to be rich; they just want to achieve what I call *financial dignity.* Financial dignity is being able to cover your financial obligations so you can sleep well at night. You can make the mortgage payment or pay the rent each month. You have health insurance for yourself and your family so that you can get decent medical care, and you can afford to go to the doctor without having to cross the border to receive medical help, as many Latinos in Southern California do. You can pay for eyeglasses and eye exams and dentist visits. (A lot of people who don't have good vision won't go to the doctor because eyeglasses aren't covered by insurance.)

Financial dignity means that you are able to send your children to decent schools. You have a little money put aside for a rainy day. You can invest each year in a 401(k) or other retirement plan. You pay your bills on time; there are no bill collectors chasing you. When you need to, you can pay for big items like furniture or appliances without having to put them on layaway or dip into your emergency fund. You can take your family on a decent vacation once a year and create some memories. You can help your brothers or sisters or parents in an emergency. You can go to a restaurant and order what you like, instead of having to choose the least expensive item on the menu. You can take your spouse to a movie once in a while. You have a decent car that doesn't break down all the time because it's so old. You can bury a loved one without having to borrow money. You can donate to your church or favorite charity. You can pay your property tax bill or other major yearly expense without having to wait for the tax refund check.

I'm sure you agree that none of these are extravagant financial goals. None of them takes a lot of money if you look at the expenses one by one. But put together, they add up to more than many people can earn working in America. And for far too many of us, the difference between financial dignity and financial desperation is only one paycheck. If either you or your spouse gets sick, has an accident, or loses your job, you can slip from dignity to desperation in a moment.

It doesn't matter if your job is blue collar or white collar, professional or manual labor, if you've been in this country for a year or forever—everyone deserves the opportunity to achieve financial dignity through his or her own efforts. But for many people, the only means of achieving financial dignity is to start a business. For them, becoming an entrepreneur isn't a luxury—it's a necessity born of their need for a better life.

When my father came to Los Angeles, he didn't have any idea of creating a business; he just wanted to earn a better living for himself and his family. But he found himself stuck in a low-paying job with little or no opportunity for advancement. And he also lacked the formal education that could have landed him a higher-paid manager or supervisor position. So out of necessity, he created his own business.

Nowadays I see people all the time caught in the same situation as my dad. They are working several jobs just to support their families, and they do not have the time or resources to get the education they need. As a result, they do not become professionals, they do not become executives, and they do not move up in the corporate world. They are stuck in low paying, service sector "McJobs" that provide little income and even less respect. Their lack of education forces them to go out and create their own solutions to produce more income. The only way most of them can see to make more money and provide their families with a better quality of life is to start their own small businesses.

What my father did have, and what so many immigrants have, was the drive to succeed and the willingness to work hard. More important, he had optimism. He dared to dream of creating something better for himself and his family. That same dream brings people to our country every day. Dreaming of a better life is the fuel that propels every would-be entrepreneur.

If you're reading this book, I believe you, too, have dared to dream. You've either created your small business already, or you've been inspired or motivated to think about starting one in the future. If so, congratulations! You have completed the most important step of all: you've opened the door to the possibility of a new, better, different future for you and your family. You believe enough in yourself and your abilities to consider taking on what can be one of the biggest decisions of your life—to leave the security of a job to create something on your own.

I urge you not to take this step lightly, because it will mean a lot of hard work and sacrifice. However, there are ways you can improve your odds of success and, more important, your odds of having a great business and having a life at the same time. This book is designed to show you some key ideas, beliefs, and strategies for starting and running a small business that will (1) provide you with a good income, (2) give you enormous satisfaction both in terms of the work you do and how your work fits into the rest of your life, and (3) become a valuable asset that you can sell when you're ready to move on. But in the same way your small business starts with a dream, creating that small business starts with an understanding of what it will take to make the transition from who you see yourself as right now to the small business owner you can become.

THE LADDER OF WEALTH

When I teach people about attaining financial greatness, I show them something I call the Ladder of Wealth. (Robert Kiyosaki uses a version of this ladder in his book *Rich Dad, Poor Dad.*)

Most people enter the ladder at the bottom as *students, interns,* or *apprentices.* They usually make very little money, if any at all. They're investing time and energy to master a specific job or profession.

After a certain amount of time and/or demonstrated ability, they become *employees* and are paid for their work. It is possible to become financially successful as an employee, if you work really hard and put as much money as is allowed in your 401(k). But you probably will have to work a very long time and save a lot, or be in the kind of job that requires technical skill and thus pays a high hourly wage. In my dad's case, employment was never going to produce the kind of financial dignity he wanted for his family.

The next step on the Ladder of Wealth for most people is to become *managers* or *supervisors.* The company invests in you, trains you, and then promotes you, or you leave the company to become a manager or supervisor somewhere else. Managers make more money than a typical employee, but the way to wealth is pretty much the same: you keep working, put as much as you can into your retirement savings, and hope your company stays in business.

At these two levels—employee and manager—the way to wealth is through *income.* Some businesses will allow employees and managers to participate in the *equity* of the company (that is, the value of the business) by putting company stock into the individuals' retirement accounts or giving stock options or bonuses when the company does well. But for the most part, if you work for someone other than yourself, you will run into what I call the *income ceiling*: you only can make as much as the company is willing to pay you. That's why so many people are eager to do something that can generate greater rewards. (In some cases, people leave a company because they have higher standards. They look around and think, *I always wanted to do what I'm doing, I'm working hard, but the owner's never around, and the company just doesn't care about us or our product. I believe I can do it better, so I'm going to go out on my own.*)

Most people who start their own businesses choose their product or service based upon what they did in their previous jobs. They do what they were doing before, only this time they're working for themselves: they become *self-employed*. The jump from manager/supervisor to self-employment is tricky. The great news is that there's no income ceiling. The bad news is that there's no safety net, either. You are directly responsible for every cent of income you produce. You can make a lot more money, but you can make a lot *less* as well, especially at the start. You're also responsible for business taxes, Social Security, the full cost of health insurance, all retirement savings, supplies, raw materials, and so on—things that employers often provide.

The problem with self-employment is that wealth is still achieved through income rather than equity. If you're not working, there's no income; and when it's time to sell the business, there's nothing to sell because all the value of the business is represented solely by your work. Essentially, you have created another job, working for a different boss—yourself.

Showing people how to step to the next level, that of a *business owner*, is both my expertise and my passion. As a business owner, you're building something that has value in addition to what's provided by your individual efforts. You create an entity that brings in money while you're not there, allowing you to take vacations, go to your children's school and sports activities, or spend time with your spouse. You can work on making your business better instead of having to drive the truck or prepare the taxes or press the dry cleaning or sew the shirts or create whatever product or service you provide. You're also building an asset that someone eventually will want to buy or that you can pass on to your children when you retire.

There are two additional rungs on the wealth ladder: *investor* and *philanthropist*. As an investor, once you've created a small business and you're building equity, you either can put your profits in your retirement nest egg or use them to grow your business. Eventually you may do well enough to invest in another business, either your own or someone else's venture. The goal here is to continue to build equity for your future.

At the final level, *philanthropist*, you have an income stream that allows you and your family to live at the standard you desire, and you can use your additional profits to make a difference in the lives of others. Warren Buffett and Bill Gates are both superlative examples of men who have taken the fruits of their businesses and used them to do good in the world. However, in every community you can find examples of small business owners who are sponsoring schools, amateur sports teams, clinics, and charities. The good news is that you can adopt parts of the philanthropist mind-set all along the way and increase your satisfaction and fulfillment in the process. We will talk more about the joy of contribution in later chapters.

Is it possible to go from being an employee or manager directly to business owner? Can you transform your current business from self-employment to something that has life beyond your individual work? Absolutely. I believe the path to a great small business and a meaningful life is clearly marked, but it takes energy and commitment to walk it successfully. There are also many stumbling blocks, which I cover in "The 22 Temptations of a Small Business Owner" in the appendix. This book is designed to help you map out your own unique path to success, based on your values, goals, needs, desires, and life situation. If you follow its suggestions, you can reach the goal of owning a business and having a satisfying life more quickly than you ever imagined.

THE THREE M'S

When you decide to make the leap from employee or manager to small business owner, there's a lot of work to do first. You've got to figure out what business you want to start; you have to create plans for that business; you have to amass capital either from your own savings or through financing or investors; you have to figure out where to put your office or storefront or facility. There are a hundred different decisions, plans, and dreams you must implement. However, in order to be successful, I've found that the first area where you must put your efforts is the one between your ears.

Achieving financial greatness has far less to do with external resources than it does with internal ones. My early clients all came from poor families; they usually were starting their businesses on a shoestring. They'd never had the opportunity to be in environments where people learned about money and creating wealth. (Have you ever heard of lottery winners who go broke within a year? Many of them came from working-class backgrounds and had never had to manage large amounts of money, and so they lost everything.) Conversely, the clients who did create successful small businesses worked as hard on building their internal resources as they did on amassing capital and customers. They made sure they were prepared mentally to handle the challenges that would arise in their path to success.

I studied these clients to learn what made them succeed when others in similar situations were struggling. And I found that they had mastered what I call the 3 M's—*mind-set, money,* and *meaning.*

I. MIND-SET

Through the years I found that I could try to teach people about financial literacy, but unless they had the right *mind-set* they wouldn't be able to absorb the information. They had to believe that they could learn about finances and business and that, while it might not be the easiest material to master, they were as capable as the next person of being a success. Most of this book is focused on giving you the right mind-set to be able to succeed. When you have the right mind-set, it's easier to learn the lessons that will help you choose a business, design its day-to-day functions, create systems, and gather and manage your team.

2. MONEY

Each of us has beliefs about money that either support us or prevent us from taking care of what we have and then earning more. If you believe that money is the root of all evil, for instance, subconsciously you'll end up sabotaging your efforts to become wealthy. You need to recognize what money is—a means of providing a better life for you and your family—and treat it with respect.

3. MEANING

The meaning you create around starting a business will determine how hard you will work and how long you will persevere. Meaning includes all of your personal reasons for starting a business—what a business will give you, who you will be as a business owner, what it will mean for your family, your future, and your community. Meaning provides you with the inspiration and motivation to get up each day and put in the work to succeed.

When your mind-set, beliefs about money, and meaning are positive and aligned with each other, you're ready to start building your business. In part 1 of this book you'll learn more about creating the mind-set required for success. In part 2 you'll discover how to create a meaning that will propel you to build the business of your dreams.

BUILDING A SMALL BUSINESS, BIG LIFE

Every small business owner will tell you how quickly any business can become the most important thing in their world. Indeed, our American culture tells us constantly that if we're not successful at work, our lives are a failure. But it's heartbreaking to see a business eat up the life of its owner. As a business consultant, I've listened as client after client has said, "Tell me which business I should start to make the most money." I ask, "What do you like to do? What do you know?" Only to have them reply, "I just figured I'd do whatever makes the greatest amount of money." Then, five years later the same clients would come in and tell me, "Louis, the only reason I started this business was to make money so I could take better care of my family. But I'm so busy that I don't see my kids anymore. I come home at night completely exhausted. My spouse is threatening to divorce me if I don't spend more time at home. What can I do?"

Through the years, I have polled my business clients, and, even though most of them would say that they value family over everything else, more than 70 percent of them are divorced. Their businesses have given them little money, less time with their families, and even less enjoyment of life. And that's not what they want or deserve.

I want to propose something radical: *the true purpose of a business should be to give you not just more money but more life.* In my definition, a big life is one in which you have money, time, love, and health to share with the people you love. Success isn't represented only by money, but also by being wealthy in all of the things that matter. Time with your family. A healthy body and mind. Rich relationships with colleagues and friends. A home environment that makes you happy the moment you walk through the door. A spiritual connection with something greater than yourself. Feeling like you're contributing not just to yourself and the people you love, but perhaps making a difference in the lives of those less fortunate. When we're truly wealthy in all of these different areas, we can say that we're living a big life that's being supported by our small business.

"Small business, big life" is shorthand for putting your small business into perspective. I believe you can have a business and earn more for your family while you still have enough time for a fulfilling life. Yes, you'll still work hard. Yes, you'll probably put in a lot of hours, as well as a lot of your heart and soul, into your business. Yes, there will be times when your life will seem out of balance and you'll feel your business pulling at you when you are trying to spend time with your children or your spouse, or working on your health or your finances or all the other important areas of life.

But unlike so many people who lose everything while building their businesses, you will stand a chance of creating a healthy, productive business while keeping the rest of your life nourished, vital, and flourishing. It's not the easiest of balancing acts. But there are ways to make building a small business, big life easier along the way.

Creating a successful business and life takes planning, designing, and calculating—just like building a house. Let's say you want to add a room to your house—a sun porch, a TV room, or maybe a nursery for a new baby. You have never done any real building before, but you're pretty handy with a hammer, and you have a lot of friends who are willing to help you on weekends. You're all excited about your new room—but if you don't have clear, detailed plans for building it, how are you going to know where to start? If you don't know the kind of foundation you need or the amount of lumber, sheetrock, and nails required to put up the walls, how much time, money, and effort are you going to waste in mistakes and delays? On the other hand, if you spend a little time at the outset deciding exactly what you want and creating a plan for building it, how much easier will it be to build the room of your dreams? And if you have a seasoned architect and builder to help you design your blueprint, will your room be more likely to stand the test of time?

If you will let me, I will be the "architect" who will guide you through the process. I've been privileged to help hundreds of other small business owners and would-be entrepreneurs create blueprints for their businesses and their lives. I've seen what works, and I've seen the pitfalls. I believe that my own experience and theirs can help you achieve greater success with fewer mistakes along the way.

Just as any lasting structure must have a strong foundation, your business and life must begin with a *strong internal foundation*, which you'll learn about in part 1. I call this foundation the four cornerstones of personal greatness: truth, responsibility, awareness, and courage. Once these cornerstones are in place, you then must create a *plan* that will help you achieve the goal of building a business without sacrificing the other significant parts of your life such as your family, your health, or your connection to your community. Part 2 shows you how to create a plan based on your life goals, one that will give you more satisfaction and success as you pursue your dream of entrepreneurship. You will also learn how to organize your small business around the important functions every business must fulfill on a day-to-day basis to be successful. Then you will see how you can automate these functions by setting in place systems that allow your business to operate and grow more efficiently and effectively.

With the daily functions of your business clearly delineated, and systems in place to make those functions automatic, you as the business owner can spend time on your other life goals. You'll worry less and accomplish more. Your kids will know who you are because you help them with their homework and go to their games and recitals. You'll be able to take weekends off to spend with your spouse. You'll have time to exercise and take care of your health. At work you will focus on the things that you as the owner must oversee, create, or accomplish. Your chances of success will increase, and your satisfaction with both your business and life will go through the roof.

This book shows you how to build a business from the inside out. It's not a manual that will teach you how to write a business plan, get financing, fill out forms, build inventory, hire employees, or invest in your business. In appendix D, you'll find a list of books, Web sites, and organizations to help you with the "how-to" part of creating and running a business. I've also given you some of the tools my clients and I use to make our businesses and our lives more successful. In appendix A, you'll find a process for creating and attaining goals. Appendix B lists twenty-two temptations that entrepreneurs face in starting and running their businesses, along with some suggestions for avoiding them. Appendix C gives you a basic outline for planning your personal financial future, independent of your business. My hope is that these appendices will give you additional tools that will help ensure your success as you launch and grow your small business.

I've been very fortunate to have my father as my inspiration. When I was growing up in the barrio, he would tell me, "You have gifts, my son— and you have a responsibility to use them." He always let me know that I could do anything I believed I could accomplish. Even though he had a limited education, he watched with pride as I went off to college. He was prouder still when I came back to the barrio and started my own small business, helping people do what he had done so long ago—to dare to build a better future for himself and his family. I watched as he turned his dream into a reality; and I've managed to turn my own dreams of small business ownership into a thriving enterprise. Now I'm privileged to help others do the same.

But more than as a businessman, my dad was my role model of someone who knew about the importance of a big life. He's no one you would notice walking down the street, but he always took time for me and my brother and sister. He has loved my mother for forty-six years, he loves his grandchildren, he has tons of friends, and he has made a difference in the lives of his customers, his employees, his community, and his family. His business always stayed small, but his life has been lived large.

By applying some key secrets of business building, it's possible for you, too, to live a great life and have a great small business. If you are ready, let's start building your future together.

PART 1

The Four Cornerstones
of Personal Greatness

Who you are at your core—the strength of your personal values—will determine the business you build and the life you are able to live. We have all seen what happens when a business or a person lacks a strong foundation of personal values. The temptation to cut corners or increase profits by slightly shady means is all around us. But while such behavior may produce short-term gain, I have found that it inevitably comes back to haunt you, if not professionally then personally. The owner of the corner store gets caught selling cigarettes to minors and pays huge fines. The clothing manufacturer can't get a loan because she's hiding her real net worth to avoid paying taxes. The auto mechanic gets a reputation for shoddy work and loses business to a more ethical competitor down the street.

Certainly we've all seen companies and individuals who have profited from cheating their clients and deluding the public. However, as Jesus said in one of his parables, a foolish man who builds his house on sand will watch it fall when the wind and the waves batter it. To build a business that will withstand the challenges of life, you first must create a strong foundation of ethical values and then stick to those values no matter how great the temptation to let them go.

I have identified four values or cornerstones that are essential to building both a strong small business and a big life. In the same way that you must pour your foundation before starting to build a house, you must have these four cornerstones in place before you begin designing your business and your life. Each cornerstone is described in its own chapter.

(1) *Truth*—This is not just honesty in your personal dealings (which should be a given) but equally important, honesty with yourself. It's far too easy to delude yourself about your reasons for starting a business, how difficult the path may be, the amount of resources you will need, and whether you're equipped mentally and emotionally to make a success of your venture. In chapter 2 we'll talk about some of the hard truths of starting a small business.

(2) *Responsibility*—You must take responsibility for all aspects of your business. This isn't easy, as almost every single day there will be circumstances and events that are beyond your control. You can't control an employee's illness or a water main break on your street that shuts down your offices. Although you can do everything in your power to market to the right people and publicize your product, you can't control the number of customers who walk in your door. You must learn to deal responsibly and resourcefully with the obstacles you will face. In chapter 3 you'll learn several secrets for taking responsibility and dealing with events resourcefully instead of reacting to them on impulse or meekly suffering the consequences.

(3) *Awareness*—We all have our blind spots, areas of our personalities or our businesses that we simply can't see. You need to become aware of your strengths and weaknesses so that you can increase the one and mitigate the other. You also need to become aware of any parts of your entrepreneurial mind-set that may hold you back from success, so you can adopt new beliefs that will support you. Finally, you must become aware of the ways your daily actions and decisions about your character, standards, morals, and ethics

directly affect your potential for success. In chapter 4, you will see how awareness helps you make the right choices that will build a strong foundation for personal and professional success.

(4) *Courage*—Most people want to live an upright life and be successful in business, but all too often they lack the courage to make the hard choices that would give them both. It takes courage to create something from nothing, which is what every small business owner does. It takes courage to keep a dream alive in the face of ongoing obstacles. It takes courage to admit when you're wrong. In chapter 5, you'll learn how to look your weaknesses straight in the eye, and to have the courage to change when needed.

I use the abbreviation T.R.A.C. for these cornerstones because these values keep us on "track" as we go about creating and building a business. Keep these principles in mind, use them daily, and you will find you can build a stronger business—and a life—that will withstand the test of time.

2

Truth

Truth should be the bedrock of business, yet in far too many circumstances we've built our businesses on shaky ground. In today's business climate, it seems people no longer expect the truth from others. They expect salespeople to fudge about delivery dates and product features. They aren't surprised when they have to send something back for a recall because the company didn't tell the truth about problems with a new product. They look with suspicion at sales numbers and earnings reports and all the other information that is supposed to give an accurate picture of a business's fiscal health. And in their own lives, they take a few deductions on their personal income tax return that they know aren't quite accurate, but they figure they can get away with it.

This climate of "near-truth" has produced cynicism, financial pain, and a culture of getting away with things rather than holding to a standard of honesty. Yet think about the people and businesses you admire and enjoy doing business with. We've all heard the stories about George Washington and the cherry tree, and "Honest Abe" Lincoln. We know how much we admire companies that stand up and tell the truth in difficult circumstances.

When Tylenol was tampered with back in the 1970s, Johnson & Johnson pulled every bottle from the shelves and launched a major campaign to tell people what they were doing to make sure their medicines would be safe in the future. Contrast that to the battle cigarette companies have been fighting for decades, trying to convince us that they didn't know cigarettes were bad for us! Honesty should be the currency of business, and it should be our personal standard as well.

Sometimes the most difficult person to tell the truth to is yourself. We all have a certain self-image that we need to preserve in order to feel good. If something goes against that self-image, we usually do our best to deny it, ignore it, or delay dealing with it. Yet when it comes to starting a small business, you need to be painfully honest with yourself about everything—your motives, your resources, your timeline, your expectations, your fears, your hopes, and your knowledge. You have to know where you're starting from before you can plan where you're going.

Think of your small business like a trip into uncharted territory (which it is, to a degree—every small business is unique and will require different resources to suit individual circumstances). If you were getting ready to take such a trip, what would you need to do before setting out? You would need to put together the supplies and the team to take the trip. You would need a map and, perhaps, a guide. One of the smartest things you would do is to have a checklist of resources. You would write down everything you already have (flashlight, hiking shoes, insect repellent) and everything you need to acquire (climbing ropes, a good map, camping gear, food, and so on).

Then you would include anything you need to do or learn before undertaking such a trip. If you have never done any climbing, for instance, you might take some lessons. If you're not in shape, you might start a conditioning program so that you'll be able to hike for days at a time. In order to be successful, you will have to be truthful about your strengths and weaknesses, and you will need to take action to make sure you have all the external and internal resources to make a success of your trip. Now, you could tell yourself, "I know I have everything I'll need!" and just wing it without a list, but you'd stand a pretty good chance of forgetting something, ignoring something important, or worse, failing because you didn't prepare well enough for the journey.

When you are thinking about starting a business, you need to put together the same kind of list. This list, however, doesn't enumerate the material things you will need—it's more personal than that. You need to catalog the internal and external resources you will need to become an entrepreneur. This can be called a personal inventory, a strengths and weaknesses list, or a "What I Have/What I Need" roster. Whatever you call it, you need to take the time to tell the truth about exactly what will be required of you and by you to start your business.

YOUR PERSONAL INVENTORY

Take a few moments to do this now. Get a blank piece of paper, and put your name at the top. Draw a line down the middle of the page. On one side, put the heading, "To start my business, I will need . . ." Now, start brainstorming everything that you could need to start a business. List *physical things* like inventory, a building, and so on. List human resources like employees, customers, suppliers, and consultants. Then move on to *intangible things*— emotions like courage, persistence, creativity, optimism, and honesty. Think about this business in good times and bad. What resources would you need when the you-know-what hits the fan? What other resources would you need if your business grows rapidly and you have to expand before you think you're ready? This kind of brainstorming is not the creative/goal-setting/visionary kind. It's more of the "heading into the wilderness/what to do if I run into bears or wildcats or get lost" truth telling.

Once you've come up with your resources list, it's time to be painfully honest about yourself and what you can bring to the table. On the other side of your piece of paper, put the heading, "My resources are . . ." Make a list of every possible *resource* you already possess. Do you have a good credit record? A house on which you can take a second mortgage to finance your business? Assets you can sell? Friends who will invest with you? Family who can help you? What skills and knowledge do you have? Have you run a business before? Can you create a balance sheet? Run a computer? Market a product? Do you have a database of possible clients? Can you run your business from home until it grows a little more?

Next, list your *personal strengths*—emotions and qualities that will help you succeed. Are you determined? Creative? A natural leader? Do you get things done quickly? Are you thorough?

Finally, what *weaknesses* will you need to handle in one way or another? Do you have trouble finishing projects on time? Is this your first time starting a business? Do you hate math and figures? Are you a lousy salesperson? Are you shy or nervous when it comes to talking about your business? Are you better at details than the big picture, or the other way around?

If you wish, you can enlist close friends or family members to help you with this list, but only if you're willing to ask them to be completely honest with you. Your goal is not to get a pretty picture. Instead, you want to formulate a realistic assessment of the truth about yourself and the business you wish to create.

All progress starts by telling the truth, no matter how painful. The truth may hurt, the truth may offend, but the truth will set you free. More important, it will free you to build a business based on accurate information and realistic assessments instead of false hopes and pipe dreams.

TELLING THE TRUTH ABOUT SMALL BUSINESS

I said in chapter 1 that small business is as much a part of the American dream as owning a home. Unfortunately, all too often the dream of a small business is far removed from the reality of creating and running one. When I work with entrepreneurs, I start by telling them the truth about their odds of succeeding. The statistics are pretty grim. According to the U.S. Department of Labor and other business research organizations, from 67 percent to 80 percent of most small business start-ups fail within the first five years. Of the businesses that survive, 80 percent fail within the next five years. *Only four out of one hundred small businesses are still around after ten years.* You have to be either very lucky or very smart to stand a chance of succeeding.

The truth is that a large part of your success is determined not by the market but by you. Therefore, you also must tell the truth about your personal finances. The hard truth is that most people in the world end up dead broke. According to a 2002 survey, 40 percent of Americans say they live beyond their means. Between 25 and 56 million Americans don't have bank accounts in insured, mainstream financial institutions. In 2005, the savings rate in the United States was *minus* 0.5 percent—the lowest it has been since the Great Depression of the 1930s. That means most people spend more than they earn and have to dip into savings or borrow to make ends meet.

In 2002, more people filed for bankruptcy in the U.S. than graduated from college that same year. More than 1.6 million people filed for personal bankruptcy in 2003. While most individuals will spend millions of dollars over their lifetimes, very few have bothered to learn anything about finance, investing, and taking care of their money. Even though you can go on the Internet and find more than 180,000 pages on how to invest in retirement plans for many companies, people still aren't putting money aside for retirement, much less creating a nest egg to invest in a new business.

The truth is that owning a small business will require many of the same qualities and disciplines that you need when dealing with the money you're earning from a job. You are going to have to save, invest wisely, take out loans, make payments on time, and put off the instant gratification of buying something on credit that you don't need and invest that money into your business instead. On top of all that, you are going to need to bill clients or collect receipts from sales, pay quarterly taxes, pay employee salaries and benefits, and more.

Before you think of opening a small business, make sure your personal finances are in order. You don't need tens of thousands of dollars in the bank (although it wouldn't hurt to have some cash set aside for emergencies), but you do need to be able to handle money and develop the financial habits that will help you keep your small business alive when the going gets tough.

On the flip side, the truth is that building and owning a small business is a great way to create a more prosperous life for you and your family. I believe it's one of the few ways that someone with the right mind-set, the right systems, and the right team can raise themselves up from subsistence to financial security to prosperity.

Let's take a look at three common reasons to start a business and tell the truth about each one.

REASON #1: PEOPLE WANT TO MAKE MORE MONEY.
At the beginning of building their businesses, most owners usually make *less* money than their employees. In fact, if you take the total number of hours an owner works and divide that by the paycheck he or she brings home, some new business owners earn less than minimum wage.

Small businesses are like children: they require a huge investment up front. Like a baby, you have to do everything for your small business at the beginning, and there are always more expenses than you could ever antici-pate. As your business grows, it almost always will require that you put in *more* money before you can reap the rewards of your investment. Even when your business starts producing income, often you need to put any profits back into the business if you want it to expand.

While the following truth may be unpleasant, I have to be honest about the viability of multilevel marketing (MLM) businesses. I'm not knocking multilevel marketing as a way to bring in some extra cash. But many people go into multilevel marketing thinking that they will build a business that can bring them tens of thousands of dollars a month. In the early days of my financial planning business, I had a lot of clients who came to me to have their taxes prepared, and they were all excited about the MLM they'd just joined. They would say with pride, "Next year I'll bet my income will be over $100,000 from this business. In fact, why don't you join me?" I would smile and reply, "Let's see how you're doing at the end of the year." But when they brought in their tax forms the following April, their income hadn't increased. When I asked my clients about this, they almost always had the same excuse: "I didn't put enough time and effort into it. But there are lots of people who are making millions. . . ." The truth is that in close to twenty years, I've rarely seen anyone who's made more than $3,000 a year from an MLM business.

Are there people who have done extremely well with multilevel marketing? Of course. But the ones who succeed with MLM treat it like a business rather than self-employment or a part-time hobby. As we said in chapter 1, there's a difference between owning a business and being self-employed. Your goal with multilevel marketing is to create a business that is greater than your own efforts. To do that, you need to develop the skills to run a successful business and apply those skills from the very start. If you're willing to put in the time, energy, and effort, and to treat your business like a business, you'll have a much better chance of doing well in MLM or any other venture.

The truth is that a small business can give you more money, but only after a significant investment of your time, energy, capital, and focus. And even then you might not make it. However, I believe that if you utilize the principles in this book, you stand a better chance of being one of the four businesses out of a hundred that will be around in ten years' time.

REASON #2: PEOPLE WANT MORE CONTROL OVER THEIR DESTINY, RATHER THAN BEING DEPENDENT FOR THEIR SUCCESS ON SOMEONE ELSE.

The truth is that you can do everything right and circumstances can still be against you. You open a new coffee shop and Starbucks moves in across the street. You have a great new line of software and find out at the last minute that someone else has created a better version of the same application. You create a new cantaloupe diet that sweeps the nation—until doctors discover that eating too much cantaloupe turns some people orange! You can plan for every eventuality, but sometimes your business will still go belly-up.

As we discuss in the next chapter, you can't control everything, but there is a lot that *is* in your control. You need to take responsibility for your efforts, for knowing your market, for preparing to handle most contingencies, and for supporting your team to the best of your ability. Only then will you be prepared to handle the circumstances that are beyond your control.

The truth is that even when your business is flourishing, you will always depend on others for your success. Many business owners will tell you that they feel a greater responsibility to their employees or investors than they ever did to their bosses. In addition, as a business owner you are responsible to your clients, customers, suppliers, and vendors. You are responsible to the landlord of your place of business, to the bank or any other institution that has loaned you money, and to many others. Do you control your destiny? Certainly—but in return you have just acquired a lot more responsibility. We'll talk about responsibility in the next chapter, and about how to create a great team in chapter 10.

REASON #3: PEOPLE WANT TO HAVE MORE TIME FOR THEIR FAMILIES.

The truth is that most small business owners spend *less* time with their families. When was the last time you met an entrepreneur who was working fewer than forty hours a week? As I said earlier, a new business is just like a new baby, and it will require at least as much of your time, energy, and effort. Unfortunately, that will mean less time for your family and yourself. And there are consequences to neglecting your important relationships. According to statistics, 57 percent of marriages in the United States end in divorce. While I haven't found any statistics on the divorce rate among small business owners, I have done a survey among our clients. We're a financial planning firm that caters to small business owners, and of our one thousand clients, approximately *74 percent* have been divorced at least once.

Of course, it's not just spouses who are shortchanged by the time demands of a small business. In talking to my brother, who is eleven years younger than I am, it sounds as if we had completely different fathers. When I was in elementary school, my dad would come home from his job at the lighting company around 4:30, and we would go off to the park to shoot hoops or play catch. Dad came to see my basketball games; he helped me with my homework; above all, he was physically present. But just about the time my brother was born, Dad started his ironworking business. He would come home around 7:30 P.M., exhausted. He rarely had time to play baseball with my brother or to go to the park. In fact, I always saw more of my dad than my brother did because from the time I was eleven years old I was helping him in the business.

Several years ago, a prominent owner of a real estate company was given a small business lifetime achievement award. He was a wonderful pillar in the community, constantly lending a hand to others. But something struck me as suspicious when I saw him giving his award speech: he was sad instead of happy. While he thanked everyone involved, he kept showing his award to his family, who were sitting at a table next to the stage. He told his two grown-up daughters that he was sorry for never being around while they were little. "I hope you can see how important my work was to me. I will make time for you now," he said.

Unfortunately, at that point his daughters were in their late forties. While their dad was taking care of the urgent things for his business, he also was missing class plays, school conferences, and soccer games. He hadn't been around for his daughters' first dates, to help them with homework, to look at them with pride as they went off to the senior prom. His daughters loved their father and respected him; they just didn't know him. By the time he had time for them, it was too late to create the memories that last a lifetime.

Recently I attended a church service close to where I live, and I heard Pastor Rick Warren (author of *The Purpose-Driven Life*) say that if the devil doesn't make you bad, he makes you busy. The truth is that a small business will engulf you in busy-ness if you don't create a new way of being in it. I know this personally: I was engulfed by busy-ness when building my own financial planning firm. I had to go through a divorce, health problems, and much more before I decided that there had to be a better way.

The truth is that the real purpose of a small business should be to give you more life, not less; more time with your family, not less; more wealth, not less; and more control, not less. The second part of this book is designed to show you how to design and run your small business so you can make this truth the one that you are living. They don't teach this in business school. I have an MBA from a prestigious college, and they failed to teach me these principles. But I care about entrepreneurs, and I want them to succeed beyond their wildest dreams, which to me means having both a successful small business and a happy life outside of it.

Here is the final truth: when everything is said and done, we're all going to end up in the same place, and that's six feet under. As we will discuss in chapter 6, only when you decide what's really important in your life can you discover the truth of how your small business will help you create it. Then you can design a business that's part of your life rather than the other way around. And before you're planted in that cemetery plot, you will be grateful for what your business has given you instead of being regretful for what you paid for it in time, money, and effort.

3

Responsibility

In my seminars, I tell a story about Maria and Roberto. Roberto is on his deathbed and his wife, Maria, is there with him. He says to her, "Maria, I love you so much. You've always been there for me. You were with me when I lost my job. You were with me when the house burned down accidentally and we had to rebuild it. You were with me when my back went out and I couldn't walk for six months. You were with me when our daughter married the Hell's Angel. You were with me when she left him and moved back in with her three kids. You've been with me through some of the toughest times a man could experience." Then he thinks for a moment and says, "Come to think of it, maybe you're the one that brought me all the bad luck!"

The surest way to achieve success in life and in business is taking personal responsibility for both. Unfortunately, I run across so many people who blame everyone *but* themselves. Before I start working with any business owner, I ask them two questions: (1) Who controls your destiny? (2) Why is your life or business not working? Here are a few of the responses I hear to the first question:

"God controls my destiny."

"My wife controls my destiny."

"My kids control my destiny."

"My parents control my destiny."

"My boss controls my destiny."

"The government controls my destiny."

"The shortage of time, money, or experience controls my destiny."

There are many other excuses (some so weird that I didn't write them here because you wouldn't believe me). But they all boil down to the concept of *fatalism*. Fatalism is the belief that someone or something other than you controls your destiny. Unfortunately, with this belief you give up the right to live the life of your dreams. Success requires that you stand up and take responsibility for your life and your actions. You can't just wait for God or the bank or your friends or whomever to give you what you need. You have to take the actions that will create what you desire. As someone once told me, "God made the fish and the nets, but he didn't put the fish *in* the nets." You need to cast the net and catch the fish.

For most people, the answer to the second question ("Why is your life or business not working?") almost always describes circumstances outside themselves. "My life's not working because I don't have enough time for my family; I'm working so hard to get the business going." "My business isn't working because we don't have enough customers." "I've been sick." "My kids have been sick." "Our competition is making an aggressive push into our market." I could count on the fingers of one hand the number of times I've heard someone say, "It's my fault things aren't working." Only when you take responsibility for how your life and business are functioning can you actually do something to make them both better.

Taking responsibility means making the hard choices and doing the difficult things that will be required of you as a business owner. It's never enjoyable to have to reprimand or fire someone. It's not easy to hold sales-people accountable for producing results, to ask someone to stay late to correct a mistake, or to be the "bad guy" who insists on keeping to the budget. But it's your job.

President Harry Truman had a sign on his desk in the Oval Office: "The buck stops here." As the owner of the business, your job is to take ultimate responsibility for your business and its workings. The buck stops with you. If you need to lay off staff because of a slowdown in your business, you should never expect your human resources person or your store supervisor to take the heat when it comes to sitting down with people and telling them they no longer have jobs. It's not the responsibility of your shop foreman to make the decision about who gets fired. Yes, your manager or HR person or foreman can make recommendations, but let it be your decision. You're the one who gets both the credit and blame at the end of the day, so you might as well take responsibility for whatever is producing both.

You also have to be willing to take action immediately. Waiting for things to work out is often the worst thing you can do. How many businesses have folded simply because the owners were waiting for things to work out? Truly responsible owners are proactive. They won't ask someone else to do the hard jobs, and they won't wait to make the tough choices. In the same way that everyone has to take responsibility for his or her job, you have to take responsibility for your job as the owner. And that means tough choices, made proactively, and executed in a timely fashion.

THE PERSONAL RESPONSIBILITY FORMULA

When you're ready and willing to step up to the plate and take responsibility for yourself and your business, how do you know what choices to make? Especially in difficult situations or emergencies, when people are looking at you as the owner and asking, "What should we do?" how can you put aside your emotions and make choices that you won't regret?

Years ago, I heard author Jack Canfield describe a personal responsibility formula at one of his seminars. This personal responsibility formula has changed my life since the first time I heard it. It looks like this:

$$E \text{ (events)} + R \text{ (your response)} = O \text{ (outcome)}$$

I believe this formula is an accurate representation of life. Events happen—they happen to you, to the people around you, to your business, to your country, to the world. You have little to no control over most of the events in your life. However, you do control your *response* to those events. Notice I say "response," not reaction. A reaction is a knee-jerk response (with emphasis on the "jerk"). There's no thought or analysis; often there's a lot of negative emotion in a reaction.

To understand the difference between responding and reacting, imagine that you have an itchy rash. You go to the dermatologist, and she gives you a prescription for medication. A couple of days later, you go back to the doctor. If she says you are *responding* to the medication, it means you are getting better. However, if she tells you that you are *reacting* to the medication, you know that you are not getting better; in fact, usually you are getting worse.

Responsibility is the ability to respond rather than react. You are making a conscious choice to behave in a way that will move you closer to your ideal outcome. But what do most people do when faced with a problem? They react. When you respond to events rather than react to them, you've taken a moment to think about the event and decide the best way to handle it. You realize that, while you can't control events, you can control your thoughts, attitudes, choices, and decisions. You can lower the intensity of any negative emotion and instead take the actions that will produce the outcome you want. You're in control of your response to the event, instead of blindly reacting to it.

One of the best ways to respond to events instead of reacting is to focus on your ideal outcome. For example, you have a long commute every morning and you know that eventually there will probably be an accident or unexpected road construction that may slow traffic to a crawl. It's Monday morning and you have a full day ahead of you, and the freeway's jammed. If you're reacting to the event, you probably get mad or frustrated or worse. You spend the extra hour fuming, honking your horn, and yelling at the other drivers. By the time you get to work you're in a bad mood, and you make others around you miserable.

But what if you take responsibility and prepare for this almost-certain event? You might decide to have a book on tape or a soothing CD in the car to listen to while you are stuck in traffic. I hook my iPod to my car radio and listen to comedy. There's nothing like coming into the office smiling! That's a much better outcome than making others feel lousy for no fault of their own.

Let me share with you just one of many stories of how this formula has made my life better. I came home one Friday from a very exhausting book tour. My family and I like to make Friday a "family date" night, and we usually go to the movies or out to dinner. But I was so exhausted that I excused myself. I told my family they should go to dinner without me—I just wanted to stay home and rest. My wife, who knows my workshop material almost better than I do, gently reminded me of the personal responsibility formula as she and the kids were jumping into the car. Then my youngest daughter, Aubrey, said that she had been waiting for our dinner date all week and that she really missed me. She also reminded me that I always tell people that life is about creating memories.

Boy, was that a wake-up call! She was right. I remembered the responsibility formula. My ideal *outcome* was to have a wonderful time with my family. The *event* was coming home exhausted. I was reacting to my current situation instead of taking responsibility for my outcome. My *response* was to get off the couch and take my family out to dinner. How did the evening end? We had a great time.

What are some times in your life where you reacted in a less-than-resourceful way? What could you have done differently? How could you have responded to the situation and made it better? What are some of the problems that are likely to arise when you start your small business? How can you create a plan for responding to these opportunities instead of reacting to them?

Winston Churchill once said, "The price of greatness is responsibility." I believe the price of entrepreneurship is personal responsibility. You must decide if you are willing to direct your thoughts and emotions, to respond to events rather than react to them, to focus on your ideal outcomes, and to make sure your choices are leading you toward those outcomes. Only then will you be ready to build both a great small business and a very big life.

4

Awareness

Recently I was working with a client who owns three Woman, Infant, and Children (WIC) government stores, where people buy basic supplies like diapers, milk, cheese, and bread. This lady has only a limited education, and yet she makes a six-figure income. She was getting ready to open a health food store, but she was frustrated because she wasn't able to keep her employees happy. "I'm giving them everything. I help them out. I don't understand why they're threatening to quit," she said.

When I looked at her employees, however, it was easy to see that *she* was the problem! Like many small businesses, her company had owners and employees, but no management. As the owner, she paid her people minimum wage, and she often asked them to work overtime, but she didn't pay them the time-and-a-half required by law. She also had brought in two of her cousins to work at the stores and treated them better than the other employees. There was a lot of nepotism and favoritism going on. She was trying to help her people but was not being fair and consistent; she would make a different decision for each person who approached her. When we pointed out the problems these policies had caused, her response was, "I had no idea."

Awareness is the third cornerstone of personal greatness. A lot of times people go into business because they see it as a way to make money or to fulfill their passions, but they don't have the skills to run part of the business. Worse yet, they don't even *know* that they don't have the skills. This is where awareness comes in. Awareness is different from telling the truth (which we talked about in chapter 2). With truth, you face hard facts that you already know but don't want to deal with. In awareness, you are noticing things that haven't even been on your radar before. You can't change what you don't acknowledge, and if you can't see the problem, then how can you acknowledge it and change it?

Imagine getting into an unfamiliar rental car. You adjust the seat and fiddle with the mirrors so you can drive comfortably and safely. But when you pull out into the road and try to merge into traffic, you hear a very loud "HONK!" from the other lane. You turn your head and see a small car in the lane next to you. The car was in your blind spot. Because you weren't familiar with the rental car you had no idea where its blind spot was, and your ignorance nearly caused an accident.

In the same way that almost all cars have blind spots, most of us have personal and professional blind spots. These are traits and qualities that we're not even aware of, and they may cause a problem. Many small business owners are trying to drive the "car" of their small business not realizing they have a huge blind spot in a certain area. For example, you may think you're taking great care of your customers, but you don't realize that your return policies are difficult and frustrating for them. Your data tracking may be great overall, but your bookkeeper has to go in and capture by hand the information needed for a particular report. You believe you have a great reputation for time management, but the deadlines you set are causing your employees to work weekends, creating a huge amount of stress.

In the case of the business owner described earlier, when it came to treating people equally (coupled with her lack of awareness about labor regulations), she had a blind spot that caused massive problems. Once we brought her blind spot to her attention, she was eager to change. However, sensitizing someone to a blind spot can take time, and sometimes it's more efficient to let another member of the business take over the function. So we "fired" this business owner from the day-to-day management of her employees. We promoted someone internally to manage the company, we gave raises to several of the workers, and we implemented correct compensation rules for overtime. Now the owner's making the same amount of money as before, her employees are happy, her biggest frustration is gone, and so she's happier as well.

One of the advantages of bringing in a consultant, or even asking someone you trust to observe your business, is the fresh awareness an outsider provides. Not too long ago, a man who owned an insurance agency asked me to help him. His business seemed to be doing very well, so I asked, "What do you need me for?"

"I'd like to set up systems so I can expand my business even more," he answered.

"What's the best thing you do here? Why have you grown so much over the years?" I asked.

"That's easy," he replied. "Our service is what makes the difference."

But then I asked his office manager, "What's your biggest frustration?" Guess what she answered? "Our service."

Interesting, I thought. *The owner thinks this is the best thing they do, and the office manager feels it's the biggest problem. If I start working on service, the owner's going to wonder what's going on, and if I don't address it, the employees are going to feel I'm ignoring their primary concern.*

So I asked the owner to choose his key employees, and then I asked the office staff to choose someone who was fairly new at the firm and someone else who'd been there the longest. I had the group come to my office (neutral territory). "I'm not going to mention any of you by name or even talk about specific issues you bring up, but I need to get an idea of what's really going on," I said. I made the environment very safe for them to tell me the truth because I knew they would never tell the owner (the person who cuts their paychecks) what the real problems were.

From that session, I got a very clear idea of the owner's blind spots, and I put together a generic report describing the areas of concern for the employees. I call this "elephant spotting." I'm describing the enormous "elephant" in the corner—the problem that everyone sees but no one wants to admit is there—and bringing the issue out into the open. I've done these sessions for several years in all kinds of businesses, and I learn more from this type of meeting than from any other means of gathering information. But here's the real surprise: when the owner read the report, he said, "Yeah, I knew that these areas were problems. I just didn't want to think about them."

Driving with a blind spot can cause accidents. Running a small business without an awareness of what you know, what you don't know, what you can't see, and what you don't want to see is just as dangerous.

WHAT YOUR BRAIN KNOWS— AND WHAT IT DOESN'T

I like to represent our awareness as a circle divided into six parts. (I adapted this diagram from one I learned at a personal development course.)

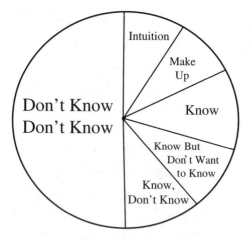

INTUITION

At the top of the circle is intuition: the stuff that we don't really know but we can sense. If you've ever made a decision based on "gut instinct" rather than rational thought, you've tapped into your intuitive sense. Intuition can be a valuable tool, as long as you don't rely on it exclusively.

THINGS WE DON'T REALLY KNOW BUT WE MAKE UP

Next to intuition is the stuff we don't know but make up. Small business owners spend a lot of time using this part of their brains. We may not know the best way to do something, but if it needs to be done we'll make it up as we go along. This tendency is useful in tight situations, but it can cause a lot of trouble if what we make up is wrong or inefficient. And there are certain circumstances—like taxes, legal issues, regulations of any kind—where making it up as you go along can get you into a lot of trouble!

WHAT WE KNOW FOR SURE

Next to that are things we know for certain. There are some things we know for sure about our businesses, our employees, and ourselves. However, we often need to check to make sure what we "know" is accurate. You could be suffering from what I call the "American Idol" syndrome. During the first few episodes of a season of *American Idol*, you see all these people auditioning. When the tough judge, Simon Cowell, asks, "Do you think you're the next American Idol?" each one of them says yes. Then you see them perform, and they're terrible. But they believe they're good because nobody's ever told them otherwise.

You see the same phenomenon in business. People come in to be interviewed or to pitch a product or service, and they have an inflated view of their abilities. It's always important to check with sources outside yourself or your business to get a more accurate portrait.

Another problem occurs when knowing is not linked with doing. How many of us "know" what we have to do to lose weight, yet we just don't do it? Or we "know" what we need to do to make our businesses even more successful, yet we won't take the necessary actions? I often encounter clients who have hired me to improve their businesses, and the first thing they do is to tell me exactly what the problem is and how to fix it. But when I ask, "If you know how to fix it, why haven't you done it?" they don't have an answer.

And when I repeat what they've told me they need to do, they spend all their time telling me how it won't work. They're not open-minded because they already "know."

It's no accident that "know" and "no" sound exactly alike—both of them keep us from looking for answers or taking the necessary action. Someone once said, "Poor people know everything; rich people *learn* everything." Even when you "know" something, you need to keep yourself open to new information and other points of view. More important, you must never let *knowing* substitute for *doing*.

WHAT WE KNOW BUT DON'T WANT TO KNOW

Other times, you know the truth inside but you're busy denying it to yourself. This is the "know but don't want to know" part of the brain. When I look in the mirror, for instance, I see the slim, young Louis Barajas of twenty years ago, even though the Louis of today is twenty pounds heavier with gray in his hair. Denial can be dangerous if it keeps you from taking action to make things better for yourself, your business, and your relationships. You handle this part by telling the truth, as we discussed in chapter 2.

In some cases, however, self-delusion can be useful. When you start a business, you'll inevitably run into naysayers and people who will discourage you from making the attempt. If you don't have enough belief in yourself to say, "I can make a go of this," you're never going to try. You have to be idealistic and realistic at the same time.

WHAT WE KNOW WE DON'T KNOW

The next part of your brain is the "I know I don't know" portion. Let me give you an example. When my stepson, Eddie, turned sixteen, we gave him my old Volvo. He drove it for a few months, then he came to me and said, "The car's jerking." I drove the car myself and told him, "It's probably the transmission."

"Can you fix it?" Eddie asked me.

"No way," I said. "I can tell you what's wrong, but I'm terrible with tools.

You need to take this to someone who knows how to repair a car." I knew that I didn't know anything about repairing car engines, and I was smart enough to take the car to someone who did.

In many small businesses, even when owners know there are things they don't know, all too often they try to do them anyway. They don't know tax law or accounting, but they try to do their own returns. They don't know workplace safety rules, and they set rules that are in violation of labor regulations. The best thing you can do when you know you don't know something is either to learn about it or to hire someone to help you. While hiring someone to help you may require a greater cash outlay at the beginning, it will save you time and money in the long run.

WHAT WE DON'T EVEN KNOW WE DON'T KNOW

The last part of your brain (and the largest) is stuff you don't even know that you don't know. When you get ready to open your first small business, almost everything falls into this category. You have no idea what you don't know, and you're not aware that you need to know it! That's why smart people do research and read and ask others about their experiences in running a business *before* they do anything else. (I hope reading this book is part of your research.)

Increasing your knowledge will help you become aware of (1) what you know, (2) what you don't know, and (3) what you will need to know in order to succeed. The life and business blueprint processes that you'll learn in part 2 will take you from "I don't know what I don't know" to "I know that I don't know." Then you can find the resources you need to gain the knowledge you'll require.

BECOMING AWARE OF
YOUR FOUR INTERNAL DRIVERS

As we said earlier, you can't change what you don't acknowledge. For most of us, the things that are the hardest to spot are internal. They are the *emotions, beliefs,* and *attitudes* that we've had for years and never really thought about. Yet these emotions, beliefs, and attitudes can dictate what we think we can and can't do, what we will or won't attempt, and even whether we feel like a success or failure regardless of our results.

To maximize your awareness of these internal drivers, you must understand

(1) your own strengths and weaknesses,

(2) your entrepreneurial mind-set,

(3) your beliefs about effort and value, money, prosperity, investment and expense, and scarcity and abundance, and

(4) your personal foundation of character, standards, morals, and ethics.

When you become aware of these internal drivers, you stand a better chance of eliminating anything that is holding you back while you build on the strengths that you already have. Your awareness in these four areas is essential in creating your personal foundation for success.

INTERNAL DRIVER #1: YOUR STRENGTHS AND WEAKNESSES

Clint Eastwood had a great line in one of his movies: "A man must know his limitations." You have to know your own limits—by this, I mean your strengths and weaknesses. When we meet with clients, we have them do several different assessments, like the test from the book *Now, Discover Your Strengths* by Marcus Buckingham and Donald Clifton. These tests help people pinpoint the kinds of tasks they enjoy and the ones they dislike, as well as the tasks they're good at and the ones they have trouble handling.

Another way to spot weaknesses is to make a "not to do" list. Ask yourself, "If things were ideal, what are the tasks that I *should not* be doing?" Most people can tell you immediately the things they either dislike or feel they don't handle well. Those tasks usually represent weaknesses. Identifying your weaknesses will allow you to hire others who excel in these areas instead of handling them (badly) yourself. We'll talk about hiring your team in chapter 10.

INTERNAL DRIVER #2: YOUR ENTREPRENEURIAL MIND-SET

In my experience, poor, struggling entrepreneurs have a different mind-set from rich, happy ones. Now you might think, *Of course! If people are poor and struggling they are going to have a different way of thinking. But if you made the poor and struggling entrepreneurs rich, they'd be happy.* However, I believe just the opposite is true. I believe that thinking precedes results. If you think like someone who's rich and happy even when you're just starting out, your results are going to be much better than if you think like someone who's poor and struggling.

It's the difference between people who see themselves as poor versus broke. Poor is permanent; broke is temporary. Let me give you an example of the difference. When Fidel Castro came to power in Cuba in 1959, many members of that country's professional class immigrated to the United States. Doctors, lawyers, CPAs, and entrepreneurs arrived with almost nothing and had to start all over again. They saw themselves as temporarily broke. Even if they weren't able to continue to practice the professions for which they were trained, usually these refugees started enterprises that allowed them to prosper in their new country. And over the years, these Cubans have been extremely successful.

On the other hand, many immigrants from other Latin American countries are the poorest of the poor. They come to the United States for better opportunities but often they bring the mind-set of poverty with them. They have always been poor, they don't see themselves as being anything but poor, and therefore they don't seek out a lot of opportunities because they don't believe that such success is possible for them. They will tell you that getting more education won't make a difference, because what good is education to a poor man? A poverty mind-set almost always guarantees that you will continue being poor. Of course, there are exceptions to both of these examples, but there is a huge difference between those who see themselves as poor versus those who see themselves as temporarily broke.

In my experience, there are five mind-sets that entrepreneurs often go through in the course of building a business. They're like steps in a staircase, and they look like this.

Survival

When you're in survival, all you're focused on is getting through the day. People who are in survival will do almost anything to succeed. Unless you plan carefully and prepare well to launch your small business, you will spend the first year or more in survival, and it won't be pretty. The best way out of survival is to make sure you have enough capital—both monetary and emotional—to carry you through until your business is on its feet.

Struggle

When you climb out of survival, you enter struggle. This is when your business is making some money, but things are still tough. Many small businesses spend years in the struggle mode, making enough to get by but not much more. To go beyond struggle, you're going to need systems, a great team, and a solid plan—all the things we'll cover in part 2. You're also going to need a compelling vision, one that will keep you emotionally on track while it inspires your team. You will learn about that in chapter 7.

Stability

The next stage is stability, and boy, does this one feel good after survival and struggle! You're producing revenue, paying your employees, maybe even growing a little bit. However, this is one of the most dangerous stages of growth for your small business because stability all too easily becomes complacency. People get comfortable, and they start to resist change. It's like being one of those folks who does the job, goes home, has dinner, and zones out in front of the television. There's no real desire for growth, and in life and in business if you're not growing, you're dying.

To get to the next stage, you must keep some of the same hunger you had in the survival and struggle stages. You have to be willing to get out of your comfort zone because change and growth are always uncomfortable. But only when you're willing to take uncomfortable risks and perhaps even drop back into struggle can you reach the next level of entrepreneurial greatness.

Success

In success, your business is humming along. You've attained your goals and perhaps exceeded them. You've built a business that you're proud of. However, now you may be facing a whole new set of challenges. For instance, many successful entrepreneurs come to me not because they want more success but because they're unhappy. "I've worked my whole life to get where I am and to build my business," they say. "Now I'm thinking, *Is this all there is?* I thought I'd be happier. What's wrong with me?" Nothing—they're just normal.

Studies have shown that once we have enough money to cover our basic needs and a little more, earning more money to buy more stuff doesn't necessarily make us happier. What *does* make us happier are close relationships, feeling like we're making a difference, and a feeling of growth or progress. The entrepreneurs I've met who are unhappy are usually focused on success to the exclusion of everything else. They never took the time to decide what they wanted once they became successful. As a result, they don't feel as if they are growing anymore, and that has led to their unhappiness.

Entrepreneurs must create business plans that project revenues and expenses for many years in advance. I would like to suggest that you do the same kind of planning for your mind-set and your emotions. What beliefs, thoughts, wishes, dreams, and feelings will you need as you climb the ladder from survival to success? Equally important, what beliefs, thoughts, wishes, dreams, and feelings will you need once you achieve your dream of a successful small business? As we will discuss in chapter 7, your vision for yourself and your business must be based in the present but tied to the future. It's the only way you will be able to make the most of your opportunities at every stage of the journey to your small business, big life.

Greatness

When you plan mentally and emotionally for your success, you'll find it's easy to reach the final level of the mind-set ladder, which I call greatness. My first book was all about achieving financial greatness, defined as an abundance of money, time, health, and love. You achieve entrepreneurial greatness when you cease to think about yourself and focus more on what you can give and what you can contribute to others. This does not mean giving away all your money, but it does mean viewing your business as an entity that can have a positive impact on yourself, your employees, your customers, your suppliers, and your community. Your success becomes a vehicle for contribution.

In 2006, Warren Buffett, who's universally recognized as one of the most successful investors of all time, announced that he was giving the balance of his $37 billion fortune to the Bill & Melinda Gates

Foundation. (Buffett had told his children many years ago that he planned to give most of his money to charity because he didn't believe in inherited wealth.) In his seventies, Buffett still goes to the office because he enjoys his work so much, but he enjoys even more the prospect of his enormous wealth doing good for others.

I would argue that following the actions of one of the most successful businessmen in the world is a pretty good strategy. Instead of thinking, *How many Ferraris can I own this year?* what if you were to ask, "How can I make more money to improve the lives of those I love and those for whom I'm responsible?" When you live at the level of greatness, you feel incredible gratitude for all you have done and created and been given. That's the feeling that true success will give you.

INTERNAL DRIVER #3: YOUR BELIEFS
Your beliefs about (a) effort and value, (b) money, (c) prosperity, (d) investment and expense, and (e) scarcity and abundance will determine whether you succeed in your small business or just struggle to get by. Let's talk about some of these beliefs so you can change the ones that may be holding you back.

A. Effort and value
Let's assume you're working forty hours a week and making $25,000 a year. If you wanted to make $50,000 a year, how many hours would you have to work? Eighty hours, right? It's a simple algebraic formula: to double your income, you'd have to double your hours worked. How many hours would you have to work to make $100,000 a year? Twice as many, that is, 160. But considering there are only 168 hours in a week, that's pretty much impossible.

So, how do you make $100,000 a year? The secret lies in the value you provide rather than the effort you expend. Are there people who work fewer than forty hours a week and make $100,000 a year? Of course. They are benefiting from the difference between effort and value.

I use a simple example of this in my seminars. "I'm going to take two people and send them out on a quest," I say. "The first person will bring back ten rocks. The second will bring back ten diamonds." After the laughter dies down, I ask, "So why is the diamond more valuable than the rock? Because we *believe* it has more value. You each have a diamond inside you—it's called your unique ability. When you create a business that allows you to tap into that unique ability, you'll be providing something that has enormous value, and people will pay you a lot more for it." We will talk more about discovering your unique abilities in chapter 7.

B. Money

If you believe that money is the root of all evil, will you work hard to earn more money? Probably not. But even if you think you believe that money's good, do you have other beliefs about money (and the people who have it) that might get in your way?

When I ask people whether they think money is good or bad, about 90 percent say that money is good. But at the same time they believe that people will do a lot of very bad things to earn money. Worse yet, those who don't have a lot of money themselves tend to believe that people with money have acquired it through illegal or immoral means. For example, when I worked in Newport Beach (a very well-to-do town in Orange County, California), whenever people saw a young Latino or African-American driving a BMW or wearing an expensive watch, they usually would say, "He must be a stockbroker or a consultant or an attorney." However, if they saw the same Latino or African-American driving a BMW or wearing a Rolex in East Los Angeles, most people would say, "He must be a criminal or a drug dealer."

To succeed in small business, you need to suspend your conflicting money beliefs. Money is neither good nor bad. Money is a magnifier; it just makes you more of who you already are. However, just like any other resource, money should be respected for the value it possesses. Money's value isn't just the numbers on the bills; it lies in what money can help you do. Money can buy a good education for your children or a comfortable home for your family; it can enable you to treat your employees better or provide you with a secure retirement. Money isn't a measure of your personal value or worth; it is a measure of the value you create for others.

C. Prosperity

If you believe in the law of attraction ("like attracts like"), you need to prepare yourself mentally and emotionally to handle prosperity. When I founded my current company, it was a struggle for the first year or so. But I told my staff, "If we want to be wealthier, we need to start thinking like wealthy people." So I arranged for everyone to learn to play golf. We got videos; everyone practiced; some of them even went out to yard sales and bought secondhand clubs. We had twenty-one-year-old kids from East Los Angeles (where sometimes a golf club is used as a weapon) out on the course, hacking away, having a great time.

Last year I had all the staff over to my home for a Christmas party, and I announced, "Tonight as part of our celebration, we're having a wine tasting." For some of my employees, this was like entering another world, but we had a great time. I printed a rating sheet from a wine magazine, and we tasted and rated Pinot Grigio, Pinot Noir, Cabernet, and other wines. It was such fun to see people who had never really thought about wine before talking about bouquets and flavors.

Having my employees learn about wine and golf is not just educating them—it's also changing the way they think about themselves. It helps them start to believe that they are worthy of good things in their lives. It expands their sense of what's possible and what they are capable of. Will they all become wine connoisseurs or golfers? Of course not. But they'll feel comfortable around people who are. And more important, they will feel better about themselves for expanding their horizons.

D. Investment and expense

In order to stretch yourself or expand your business, you must invest in both. It's all too easy, however, to put your money toward expenses (financial outlay with little or no beneficial return) rather than spending it on things that create value. Last year my wife and I went to *Librería Martínez*, a Latino bookstore in Santa Ana. The owner, Rueben Martínez, won a MacArthur "genius" grant for his work promoting literacy in the Latino community. Mr. Martínez met us at the bookstore to talk about some upcoming promotions for my book, *The Latino Journey to Financial Greatness.* There was a stack of copies of the paperback edition in both English and Spanish on a table in the front of the store.

Mr. Martínez said, "Do you see that lady looking at your book? Watch this—I'm going to sell her one."

He walked up to the woman and said, "Ma'am, have you read this book? It's changed my life. I'm opening another bookstore because of the principles in the book. It's really great."

But I noticed that while he was talking, she had turned the book over and was looking at the back cover. "She's looking for the price," I told my wife.

Sure enough, the woman interrupted Mr. Martínez and asked, "How much is it?"

"Thirteen dollars," he said.

She shook her head and put the book down. "I can't afford thirteen dollars," she said as she walked away.

That woman saw the book as an expense rather than an investment. How are you seeing things? What are you investing in, and what are you spending money on? To paraphrase my friend David Bach, the daily latte you spend three dollars on is an expense; the subscription to a trade journal that keeps you up to date on the latest advances in your business is an investment.

Investing isn't just money; it includes time and energy, too. Reading, taking classes, even thinking about your business are investments. You need to understand the difference between investments and expenses so that you will get the best return for your time, money, and energy.

E. Scarcity and abundance

When people are in survival or struggle, they tend to see resources, business, or the universe as being like a pie, with everyone competing for the biggest piece, and a larger piece for them means less for everybody else. This is the "dog-eat-dog" worldview. Those who believe this way are always focusing on what others have that they do not.

Most successful people, however, have discovered the truth that the universe is more like a pie shop than a pie; it's always producing more opportunities, more customers, more business, and more abundance. There will always be enough for anyone willing to work for it. This helps you become more creative, more resourceful, and ultimately produces better results for your life and your business.

INTERNAL DRIVER #4: YOUR PERSONAL FOUNDATION

The only way to have a small business and a big life is to develop a strong foundation to support both. The height of a building depends upon the strength of its foundation. If you try to build a ten-story office building on a foundation designed for a one-story house, the least little tremor or storm will damage the structure. The same is true of your personal foundation. You must develop the strength of character to withstand the tremors and temptations that come with your own small business.

Your personal foundation consists of (1) your character, (2) your standards, (3) your morals, and (4) your ethics. Throughout the course of your life, you're always working on your personal foundation. With each decision, each action, and each relationship, you're either shoveling dirt out and deepening your personal foundation or shoveling dirt in and making it shallower. Did you cut corners on the job you did for a client? You have just weakened your personal foundation. Did you keep a commitment even though it was difficult? You made your foundation stronger. How you treat your clients and employees and how you take care of yourself and your family also affect your personal foundation.

Many things will strengthen your personal foundation. Integrity. Making good decisions. Honoring your word. Doing what's right even when it causes you short-term pain. Courage. Telling the truth. Holding high standards for yourself and others. Forgiveness. All the virtues you've read about in the Bible and other great books will add to your foundation and make it strong enough to withstand the toughest shocks.

Conversely, the "sinkholes" that weaken your foundation include sloppiness, taking shortcuts, procrastination, lying, cheating, stealing, backstabbing, pride and ego (also known as machismo), and gossip. What I call the lottery syndrome—wanting something for nothing—saps your moral strength as well. Failing to take the right action because it will make you look bad or lose the regard of others also weakens your foundation.

As you prepare to create (or re-create) your small business, take a look at yourself and your employees, and make sure you all have strong personal foundations. Otherwise, you run the risk of producing an emotionally toxic work environment that will sap your strength and diminish your desired results. I warn you, this will be an ongoing process. You must continue to strengthen your foundation daily, and check in with your employees to make sure their foundations are strong.

As the business owner, you must lead both by example and by direction. If your character, standards, morals, and ethics are clear, certain, strong, and positive, and if you expect the same from your employees, they will get the message and either raise themselves to your level or leave. The result will be a business with a strong foundation, one that is built to last for years to come.

THE DISCIPLINE OF AWARENESS

Like the other cornerstones of personal greatness, awareness is an ongoing discipline. Every time you become aware of a blind spot, a weakness, a belief that has been holding you back, or a decision that has weakened your personal foundation, it's an opportunity for you to take action. When you take the time to examine the beliefs, thoughts, and attitudes that may be in your personal "blind spot," you can figure out ways to mitigate their effects on your business and life. Socrates said, "The unexamined life is not worth living." I believe that the unexamined life will keep you from the success you desire and deserve. The time you spend becoming aware of your beliefs, thoughts, and attitudes will help you climb the ladder from survival to greatness much faster and with far greater enjoyment.

5

Courage

Do you know people who, once they learned what they needed to do to become successful, still did not follow through? Most of the time, people don't follow through because they are experiencing fear. Fear of failure. Fear that they may be disappointed if they try hard and still fail. Fear of the unknown. Fear of change. For most people, change is difficult. They have self-doubt; they lack confidence; most of all, they lack the support system to follow through.

I know how that feels. I was a pretty decent student in high school, and I was lucky enough to have a wonderful teacher who encouraged me to go to college. He believed in me and helped me complete my application to several colleges, and I got accepted to UCLA. Now, that may not sound like a big deal to you, but it was one of the most frightening things I had ever done. I was the first person in my family to go to college. Even though I grew up less than twenty miles from UCLA, going to college was as foreign to me as going to the moon.

My senior year of high school was one of the most difficult years of my life. I knew that college was my way out of the barrio. I knew I had to file an application and do whatever it took to get in. I knew I would have to leave home and move into the dorm. But I did not know if I could compete against some of the best students in the country. I lacked confidence, and I didn't have any kind of support system. My parents didn't have a clue about college; in fact, all I knew was what I had heard from my teacher. When I packed up my stuff and moved into the dorm, it felt like I was jumping off a diving board for the first time. For most of us, that first dive is really scary. You think that you are going to drown. But somehow you find the courage to jump, and then you jump again and again until the fear becomes fun.

When you start a small business, you may feel like I did when I headed off to college. You're entering a whole new world, one where you've never been before and don't know how to navigate. You, too, may have no support system (although I hope this book will give you the information and inspiration to carry you through). If you are smart, you will do all the preparation and exercises in this book, so you'll have a lot more confidence. But ultimately, you're going to have to "jump off the diving board" and start your business. And that will require courage.

THE FOUR FACTORS OF COURAGE

I believe the best kind of courage comes when you combine the following four factors: knowledge, action, perseverance, and faith. *Knowledge* means having the right information to increase your odds of success. Once you develop the knowledge, you need to take *action*, even if you're afraid. Action is the only way to put your knowledge to work. After you begin to take action, you must develop *perseverance*. You must persist even when it seems you are not being rewarded for your efforts. Finally, you must have *faith*. You must believe in yourself and your endeavor (and perhaps in a little divine support as well).

As Ambrose Redmoon wrote, "Courage is not the absence of fear, but the judgment that something else is more important than fear." Courage is doing what you know you need to do in spite of the fear you feel. If you take the leap of faith and jump off the diving board, most times you'll hit the water clean and come up swimming.

Let's take a closer look at these four factors so that you can develop the courage you need to create a small business, big life.

1. KNOWLEDGE

To have courage, you need to understand your situation. As we said in chapter 2, starting a small business is difficult at best, but it's better to start with a realistic picture of what that business will entail. It's like knowing how deep the pool is before you jump off the diving board—you'd better have the right information so you will know if it's smart to jump!

Knowledge also entails recognizing real obstacles and challenges rather than getting caught in imaginary problems created by fear. One such obstacle may be peer pressure. I was lucky that my parents supported my decision to go to college, even though they couldn't give me any information to help me take the leap. But often when you take a leap of faith and start a new business or any other venture, the people around you will try to talk you out of it. It's like the mother in the movie *Real Women Have Curves.* Her daughter wants to go to college in New York City, but the mother tells her, "You can't go because I don't want you to get hurt." Even though the mother had never done what her daughter wants to attempt, she's still afraid for her daughter.

There was a famous study in which researchers took four monkeys and put them in a cage. On the top of this cage was a container with bananas. The researchers fed the monkeys at set intervals. When the monkeys got hungry between feedings, they would reach for the bananas that they could see on top of the cage. But as soon as they reached out, the researchers would spray the monkeys with a pressurized stream of cold water and knock the monkeys down. Every time the monkeys got hungry and reached for the bananas, they would get sprayed.

You can guess what happened. Eventually the monkeys stopped reaching for the bananas—a kind of learned helplessness set in. But the interesting part of the experiment occurred when the researchers took one of the monkeys out of the cage and put a different monkey in. The new monkey had never been sprayed with the water, so it would start to reach for the bananas when it got hungry. But the other monkeys in the cage would stop it from reaching. They didn't want the new monkey to get hurt.

The researchers kept replacing the original monkeys with new ones until all four monkeys in the cage had never been sprayed with water—but none of them would reach for the bananas. They would get hungry and look up at the bananas with longing, but they wouldn't reach, even though they didn't know what was stopping them.

Do you have a "monkey" in your life? Are people telling you not to start your business or make changes in the one you have because they don't want you to get hurt or fail? Worse yet, are you telling yourself the same story? What haven't you done because it's not in your comfort zone? What's the worst thing that could happen if you went after what you want? Knowing the possible consequences allows you to prepare for them and decide when the risks are worth it based on your own rules, not the rules that you've inherited from your family or community or peers.

Often the people you love will hold you back from attempting something new because they're afraid you will change and you won't want to be around them anymore. My wife, Angie, saw this happen when we married. My office was in East Los Angeles and Angie lived in Los Angeles, but we decided to buy a home in Irvine, close to where my two daughters lived with my ex-wife. Angie and her son, Eddie, were staying with her mother at the time, and when Angie announced that we were moving to Irvine, she got a lot of resistance. Her mother said, "You're moving to an uppity neighborhood. You're going to think you're better than us. You're not going to want to be around us anymore." Angie's family wouldn't visit or even talk to us for a while. They made our lives pretty miserable because they were afraid.

Now, we could have said, "We're going to live where we want to live. If Angie's family has a problem with that, let them deal with it." But family is very important to us both, and so I suggested we make her family feel more comfortable in our neighborhood. "Let's invite them to the house, have a barbecue, and let them meet some of our neighbors," I said. Now

Angie's family is thinking of moving to Orange County, too. Instead of reacting to their negativity, we had the courage to respond with kindness and to show them a better way, and our relationship with them is closer than ever.

When you implement changes (as I hope you will based on what you learn in this book), you're going to face resistance. Worst of all, much of the resistance will come from the people you know and care about—friends, family, and colleagues. You need to develop the strength to stand up to the people you love and the courage to pursue your dream.

2. ACTION

Knowing what to do is vital, but doing what you know is the only way to create the business of your dreams. How many people do you know who have talked for years about starting a business? Maybe they've even done some research or gone to an MLM opportunity meeting. But unless they've taken the action to start that business, and unless they're committed to taking action day in, day out, then their knowledge is worthless. Action turns knowledge into tangible reality. Without constant, persistent action, your dream of a small business will remain just that, a dream.

If starting a business is like leaping off the diving board, keeping a business going requires taking that same leap day after day after day. The good news is that courage and action are part of a self-sustaining cycle. You overcome your fear and have the courage to take action, which gives you the courage to take another action, and so on. Does it get easier? Yes and no. You lose the fear that you first had when you jumped, but now you need a new kind of courage: the kind that leads you to keep taking action no matter what. That kind of courage requires inspiration. Inspiration will help you keep taking action despite the odds.

Inspiration is the internal driver of action. It's different from motivation. Motivation is external. We are motivated by a paycheck, by deadlines, by the IRS or bills, or by a million other external things. Motivation is tied to the "how" of running your business. When you or your people are motivated, once the external pressure is gone things tend to get slack. As a consultant,

I can make a series of recommendations to improve the business, but if the business owner or employees do not understand why they're doing these things, they won't follow through. I'll go back and ask, "Have you done such-and-such?" And they will say, "No, we didn't have the time." If I hear that, I know I didn't spend enough time on *why* they had to get it done. I told them what and how, but I didn't help them discover why.

When people are working from motivation (external pressure) rather than inspiration (internal drive), you see a lot of what I call the "one-yard-line syndrome." Have you ever seen a football team that consistently gets the ball to the one-yard line but somehow they rarely score a touchdown from there? That's because the team is motivated to take action rather than inspired to make the goal. In small business, you see the same thing with projects that everyone's excited to start but somehow no one seems to finish. There is not a big enough "why" for the team members to put in the effort required to complete the job.

Inspiration comes from our own personal "why." Why do you want to create or improve your business? Wayne Dyer talks about inspiration as being "in spirit." When you're in spirit, everything goes easier. It's almost as if you're working with God, doing what you love to do. With inspiration you are able to work harder; you don't have to look at your watch. Inspiration is internal. It comes from linking a goal or objective to what is truly important to you and your people.

If your business is a part of your mission in life, if you feel it's making a difference or providing a secure financial future for your family, or if you're growing enormously as a result of what you're doing, then you are operating with the internal drive of inspiration, and you will continue to take the actions that will give you great results. We've all heard the expression "Where there's a will, there's a way." However, I believe that when there's a will to follow through, there's a "why" instead. The "why" will make you find the way. And the "why" must be personal—it should be tied to what's important to you and your employees. If you can figure out the inspiration, why you're doing something and why it's important to you, then you're going to follow through with the actions that will create success.

3. PERSEVERANCE

I read once that when Mother Teresa passed away, some of the sisters of her order went into her room to clean it. On the wall over her bed were taped several quotations from the Bible and a poem. Mother Teresa read the quotations and the poem every night before she went to sleep. Written by Kent M. Keith, this poem has inspired many people to have the courage to persevere in the toughest times. It's called "The Paradoxical Commandments."

People are illogical,
unreasonable, and
self-centered.
Love them anyway.

If you do good,
people will accuse you
of selfish ulterior motives.
Do good anyway.

If you are successful, you will win
false friends and true enemies.
Succeed anyway.

The good you do today
will be forgotten tomorrow.
Do good anyway.

Honesty and frankness
make you vulnerable.
Be honest and frank anyway.

The biggest men and women with
the biggest ideas can be shot down
by the smallest men and women

with the smallest minds.
Think big anyway.

People favor underdogs
but only follow top dogs.
Fight for a few underdogs anyway.

What you spend years building
may be destroyed overnight.
Build anyway.

People really need help
but may attack you if you do help them.
Help people anyway.

Give the world the best you have
and you'll get kicked in the teeth.
Give the world the best you have anyway.

Copyright © 2001 by Kent M. Keith.

"Doing it anyway" is an ongoing process. There will always be people who doubt your motives or put you down for your success. I spend the majority of my time educating other people about ways they can take charge of their personal finances and create a small business, and it's difficult when clients or audiences flatly say that they don't believe what I have to teach applies to them.

Recently I came home, threw my keys down, and almost cried in frustration. "Nobody wants what I have to offer," I told my wife. "I might as well just give up, for the lack of support people are giving me."

"What do you care if they support you or not?" Angie replied. "You're there to help people. Just do it anyway."

Then I looked at the door of the refrigerator and saw the copy of "The

Paradoxical Commandments" we had pasted there. I was reminded of Mother Teresa and Gandhi and Nelson Mandela and all the people in this world who struggle against enormous odds. I remembered why I was working every day—my vision of creating an economic revolution for the working class in this country. I thought of all the people whom I had helped over the years and of the hundreds of thousands who needed what I have to give.

I also thought of my father, who got up each morning to go to his own small business. Nobody cared whether he succeeded or failed except for himself, his employees, and his family. But he had a vision of the life he could create for his family, and it gave him courage. My father continues to inspire me to keep to my vision and do it anyway. As you build your own small business, let your vision inspire you. It will give you the courage you need to persevere.

4. FAITH

Faith is the belief in things unseen. In business, it often means taking action without being certain you will succeed, in the belief that you are creating something bigger and better. Faith makes courage possible in difficult circumstances. When you are first starting out, faith can be very difficult, but it's the time when you need it most.

When I left my job in Orange County, I was doing very well, earning a great income. But when I opened my business in East Los Angeles, I really struggled. In my first year, I made less than $12,000. But I worked hard at marketing to and connecting with the community, and eventually my phone started ringing. Then I had a new problem: I would be with a client and have to answer the phones at the same time. I needed to hire a receptionist. When I was at UCLA, I had been a counselor at Stevenson Junior High School in Boyle Heights, and one girl really stood out. She was a great person and really knew the community. So I called and asked if she would come work for me.

At the time she was making $7 an hour, or around $14,000 annually. Fourteen grand, and I had only made $12,000 the previous year! I thought,

If I hire her I'm in the hole $2,000. But if I don't hire her, I can't grow. I've got to have faith that this is the right decision. So I hired her. She answered the phones and scheduled appointments for me, and because she took care of that part of the business, I could see more people. Pretty soon she was doing some of the work, photocopying and assembling tax returns while I met with clients. I paid her $14,000 and then gave her a raise after six months. Yet, by the end of the year my personal income had doubled, going from $12,000 to $24,000!

Now I had a new problem. Because we were getting more clients and more business, I was working ridiculously long hours. I was caught in the small business owner's "rugged individualism" trap; I thought I had to do it all myself because I could not afford to hire someone to help me. Fortunately, I had the common sense to see how stupid that was. When tax season hit, I hired another tax preparer, paying him $12 an hour, or around $25,000 a year—more than I had made the year before. I thought, *Here we go again; I'm going to be in the red instead of the black.*

But that's how business is sometimes; you have to go against "common sense" and have faith in order to expand and grow. That year, even with another employee's salary to cover, I still made $40,000 in personal income. And because I had the extra help, I could work harder on marketing our services. That year I got my first really big client, Classic Couriers. Of course, then I had to hire someone else to help me handle the increased business!

Faith can be very scary when you're just scraping by, yet you have to invest in order to grow, even though you aren't certain it's going to work until you do it. You have to have enough faith in what you're doing to leap off the diving board, and trust that you will swim just fine.

Starting a small business is a significant undertaking for anyone. It requires enormous courage to take the leap. But when your courage is supported by knowledge, action, perseverance, and faith, you will find that you are ready to take the plunge. And with a strong personal foundation of truth, responsibility, awareness, and courage, you're ready to prepare yourself to create and build a business that will give you not just professional success but also a fulfilling life—a business that will enrich your life as well as your wallet, an entity that creates both money and meaning, something that will be personally and financially rewarding while it provides a lasting legacy for yourself and your family.

PART 2

The Five Steps to Build a Small Business, Big Life

I believe that one of the reasons so many small businesses fail is that their owners don't know what it takes either personally or professionally to make their small businesses prosper. Michael Gerber, author of *The E-Myth Revisited,* says that most folks who start small businesses aren't business people but employees having an "entrepreneurial seizure." They want what they think a small business will bring them—more money, more freedom, more control of their lives—but they aren't equipped with the basic skills every entrepreneur needs. They think they can start a business because they know how to do something—prepare taxes, for example, or build wrought iron gates, or maybe make the best tortillas this side of Mexico City.

But knowing how to do something will not make a great business; in fact, I believe it's one of the *last* things to consider when you get the entrepreneurial urge. Far more important is designing an enterprise that allows you to use your unique abilities to their fullest and then learning how to run the business of your business.

These five simple steps will help you create a business that can grow both with you and beyond you, something you're proud to own and proud to have humming along whether you're physically present or not. These five steps are part of an endless circle of success and achievement, like this:

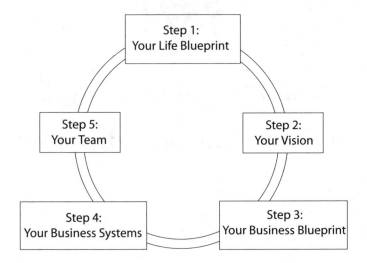

Step 1: Your Life Blueprint. Building a business is going to take a lot of time and effort, so you'd better be sure that your ROI (return on investment) is what you want it to be. I'm not talking about financial returns, but emotional ones. You could have the most successful business in the world, but if it's something you hate doing, if it goes against your core values, if it keeps you away from the things that you consider most important, or if it demands all of your life rather than giving you more life, then you won't be successful—you will just have a big business that's a burden rather than a joy.

The purpose of your business is to give you not just more money but also more life, and everyone's definition of "more life" is unique to his or her circumstances and background. If you understand your life blueprint *before* you design your business, you'll be far more likely to experience both success and satisfaction. Your life blueprint will show you how to have a life that includes your business, instead of a business that consumes your time and energy. In this step you will put your business in the context of the most important values and roles in your life. You will also discover your personal reasons for putting the time, money, and effort into starting and building your small business. This will help to ensure that your goals for your life and your reasons for starting a business are aligned, so your business will be a source of fulfillment rather than frustration.

Step 2: Your Vision. Your business should be a way for you to better express your full potential as a human being, a member of a family, and a contributor to the world. In this step you will determine your unique abilities and gifts so that you can design a business that allows you to use those abilities to their fullest. Based upon that, you can create a compelling and exciting vision for your enterprise.

When you own a small business you automatically become a leader, and leadership requires vision. You are the one who determines both the ultimate outcome of your business and the way to achieve that goal. You also must develop the ability to communicate the vision to your team. A great vision will inspire and guide you and your team every step along the way.

Step 3: Your Business Blueprint. Once you have the vision of your business, you can begin to create a plan for turning that vision into a prosperous enterprise. The final three steps focus on the *business of your business*—that is, all the various functions that must be accomplished to keep your doors open and cash flowing. You will start by building a *business blueprint:* an accurate description of exactly what is required to run your business on a day-to-day basis. This is not a "business plan" designed to get you funding. Instead, it's a description of all the different functions that must occur daily for your business to thrive. With a clear business blueprint, you'll be ready to open your doors and be successful from day one.

Step 4: Your Business Systems. Your business blueprint shows you what to do, and systems make it automatic. Setting up systems creates accountability and tracking. It will allow you as the business owner to sleep better at night and even take time off every now and then because you're confident that the business is running smoothly. In this step you will build the systems you need to streamline your business and utilize your time and effort (as well as that of your employees and outside contractors) most efficiently. Business systems are the key to having both a small business *and* a big life.

Step 5: Your Team. Whether you're a sole proprietor or you have many employees, you are the leader of a team of people who interact with your business. Your customers are a part of your team. Your employees and suppliers are as well. There are also outside professionals (bankers, accountants, lawyers, and so on) who support you in running a successful business. In this step you will learn how to recruit a world-class team and enroll them in helping you create the business of your dreams.

These five steps are designed to help you create better results and more fulfillment on the journey of creating and running your business. I believe they can provide the guidance you need to master the business of your business while keeping your eyes focused squarely on the main objective— a rich, satisfying life.

6

STEP 1: Your Life Blueprint

The Purpose of Your Business
Is to Give You More Life.

I f you had to draw a picture of the amount of time, energy, and focus you put into your life and your business, the old way of thinking about it might look like this:

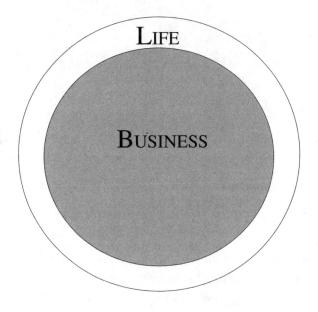

LIFE

BUSINESS

The old way is for your life to revolve around your business. The needs of the business—whether it be cash, time, energy, effort—come first. Your life—including family, health, relaxation, exercise, contribution to community, and so on—gets the leftovers. With the old way, one spouse comes to the other and says, "Honey, I'm going to start a business. Once I get it started and everything's running fine, then I'll have time for you and the kids." Five years later the spouse has filed for divorce, and the children don't know their parent anymore. That's not a recipe for long-term success.

You've got to be clear about what's really important to you and what will give you the best quality of life so that you can decide what you're willing to trade your time, money, and energy for. Your goal, your target, is to have a business and life that look more like this:

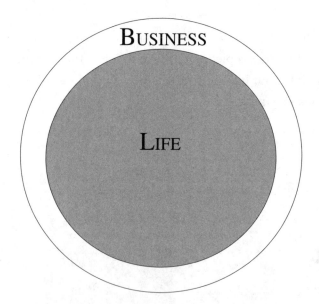

When you make your business a part of your life rather than the other way around, you start by saying, "Here are the most important roles in my life, here are the things I want to focus on, and here are the values that matter to me. How can I build a business that will let me focus on those and give me the life of my dreams?" The new way puts your life at the center of your time, energy, and effort, and your business revolves around it. The new way gives you time and energy for relationships, health, contribution, growth, and education—*and* your business. When you make these areas the focus of your life, you will come to your business refreshed, relaxed, with greater resources, and ultimately more energy, drive, and focus.

Now, I'm sure that if you already own a small business, you're thinking, *How can I make my life the primary focus of my time and energy when my business is taking every ounce of who I am?* I'm not being a Pollyanna here; I know all too well how much energy you must put into your business for it to survive and then succeed. I have that "only four out of every one hundred small businesses make it to the ten-year mark" statistic inscribed in my memory.

But I also know that far too many entrepreneurs lose sight of the reasons they start a small business in the first place. It's rarely because they're burning to go into business for themselves; instead, they want what they think a small business will give them. They believe a business will enhance their lives by helping them provide for their family, create greater financial security, allow them to contribute to their communities, and give them greater personal growth. But all too frequently they are confusing the means (the small business) with the ends (what the business will give them).

To create a small business that will give you everything you think you want from it, you first need to become crystal clear on what it is that you want. To accomplish this, you must

(1) clarify the overall goals you have for your life,

(2) understand how your business will help you attain those goals, and

(3) make sure to keep those life goals at the forefront of your entrepreneurial efforts.

When your small business is helping you fulfill your life goals, you will truly feel that you are living the big life of your dreams, one that can give you the abundance of health, wealth, time, and love that you deserve.

DESIGNING YOUR LIFE BLUEPRINT

If I gave you a million dollars to build your dream home, the first thing you would do is to hire an architect. An architect puts onto paper what your house is going to look like when it's complete. You'll see a visual representation of your million-dollar home; you'll know where the bedrooms, bathrooms, and kitchen will be located. The architect then draws blueprints that show you how to turn the picture into reality. No decent builder would work on a house without blueprints. So why should planning your life be any different?

Unfortunately, most people treat their lives like the guy who wants to build his dream house but never takes the time to make a plan or a blueprint. Instead, he just walks out to the lot with a hammer, some nails, and a bunch of building materials, and starts working. The result usually looks more like a builder's nightmare than a dream house! Your life is far more important than any house; therefore, you need to decide in advance what type of life you want and draw up plans for its creation.

Every year scores of small business owners come to see me to help them with their businesses. The first questions I'll ask them are, "How's your life? Is it working for you? Are you happy with the amount of time you're spending with your family and your kids? Are you taking care of your health?" Most of the time they'll look at me like I'm crazy. "I came here to fix my business. Why don't you ask me about what's going on there?" they will ask.

I'll tell you the reason: almost every time there's a problem in a business, it's because there's a problem with the owner's life blueprint. Of course, there may be challenges in the way the owner is running the business of the business (and we'll address that in the next few chapters), but ultimately the business is a reflection of the owner's life, and an imbalance or lack in one will affect the other. The secret to success is to create your life blueprint before you ever start developing your business plan (or, as you will see in chapter 8, your business blueprint).

When I use the term *life blueprint,* I'm not talking about a plan that indicates your career path or how many kids you want to have or how many years you want to work before you retire. I'm talking about an *interior* blueprint, based on what's truly important to you. It starts with your personal foundation of character, standards, morals, and ethics, which we talked about in part 1.

How high you're able to build the "dream house" of your life will depend on how deep your personal foundation is and how strong its cornerstones of truth, responsibility, awareness, and courage are. Once you've got your foundation in place, it's time to draw the blueprint for the "framing" and the "walls" of your life, consisting of your

(1) values,

(2) life focus areas, and

(3) essential roles.

When you know the values, life focus areas, and roles that are most important to you, then you are ready to design a business that will contribute to, rather than detract from, that high level of fulfillment.

In my experience, those who prepare a life blueprint for themselves find it much easier to create and run successful businesses because they understand how their businesses are enhancing their lives and the lives of their families. They feel a greater sense of passion about what they are doing; they can put more of themselves into the time they spend at their businesses while they also take time for relationships, exercise, church, community activities, and just plain relaxing. A life blueprint is the secret of both greater balance and greater success for anyone who wishes to start and run a business.

Creating your own life blueprint should take only a few hours—less time than most of us spend commuting or watching television or surfing the Internet every day. If you want a more detailed version of this process, I suggest you pick up *The Latino Journey to Financial Greatness*. (Even though the book uses the word *Latino* in the title, the journey to financial greatness pertains to everyone.) You also can go to my Web site, www.louisbarajas.com, to download copies of the worksheets I use with my clients.

START WITH THE END IN MIND

There's a story about Alfred Nobel, the great philanthropist and scientist. Nobel's brother passed away when Alfred Nobel was middle-aged—and the newspaper in Paris printed the obituary for the wrong brother! Alfred Nobel had the chance to read his own obituary. He was horrified to see himself called the "merchant of death" and his primary accomplishment listed as the invention of dynamite. Nobel decided he wanted to change his obituary, so in his will he created the Nobel Foundation. For more than one hundred years now, prizes have been given in his name to recognize achievement in chemistry, physics, literature, and efforts toward international peace. Alfred Nobel's name means something very different today as a result of the Nobel Prize.

How do you want your obituary to read? Stephen Covey said it more than twenty years ago: always start with the end in mind. How we view our lives at the end of our lives may be very different from our perspective when we're in the thick of starting a business. It helps to take a few steps back and evaluate where our lives are going today rather than waiting until years from now and experiencing regret about our choices.

There are various methods for looking at your life from this kind of long-term perspective. Some consultants will have you write a eulogy; others will have you imagine sitting in a rocking chair at the end of your life and thinking about your past. But I prefer thinking about today, looking at the life you've lived up to this point.

Take a piece of paper, a nice leather journal, or anything you can write on. Don't just think about these questions—it's important to write down your answers. There is magic in planning your life on paper. Write down the answers to these Life Questions.

If I knew that I had only twenty four hours to live . . .

- What would I regret not having done?

- Who would I miss most?

- Who did I fail to become?

Look at your answers to these Life Questions. What stands out to you? How many of your regrets are tied to your business? How many are linked to people you never appreciated or spent enough time with? How many amazing things did you not do because you were just too busy with work?

In my professional life as a financial planner and business consultant, I have had several very successful clients pass away. When these people knew they were dying, not one of them asked me to bring them their financial statements. Unfortunately, we often forget that life is not about "things." We get caught up in the material goals we have for ourselves and our families, and we don't remember that our kids would rather have us play catch or kick a soccer ball around with them than have us work overtime to buy a second car. We forget that our spouse would almost always rather have a "date night" instead of a piece of jewelry or a bigger television. I know I'm exaggerating and that many people work long hours just to provide their families with the basics. But all too often we think that the money we are working so hard for is more important than our time, our presence, and our love. And believe me, at the end of your life, your money will not be much consolation if you have neglected your relationships to gain it.

Sometimes people have a difficult time thinking about and articulating their answers to these Life Questions. They have an even more difficult time figuring out how to change their current circumstances so that they will have fewer regrets and feel more happiness instead. Therefore I've developed a series of exercises to help my clients clarify what's really important to them. I go through these exercises with every business consulting and financial planning client. They are the guidelines for creating a personalized life blueprint.

When you answer the following questions carefully and thoroughly, you'll have learned your own unique reasons for creating a small business. These reasons will go far beyond money, success, and personal or professional growth because they will be tied to the different aspects of life, love, and living that are most important to you. With these reasons as your guide, you will be able to look back on your life from your rocking chair or imagine reading your obituary and feel a sense of pride at your accomplishments in *every* area of life—personal, professional, relationships, and community.

I devised the following steps for creating a life blueprint by studying the works of people like Stephen Covey, Michael Gerber, and Dan Sullivan. I have been doing these steps for more than sixteen years, and I can honestly tell you that they can have a profound effect on your life.

Please follow the sequence of steps as outlined in this chapter, and *write* your answers—don't just think about them. Writing puts your thoughts into a far more tangible form, giving them a reality they don't possess when they're just in your head. I hate it when somebody says, "Trust me," but trust me just this one time. Get yourself a journal or notebook, or use the forms in this chapter, and write the answers down.

YOUR VALUES QUESTIONNAIRE

Let's start with your *values:* the emotions or relationships that are most important to you. When we are conscious of our values, they act like a compass, guiding us as we answer some of life's most important questions. Our values determine what we will or won't do. For instance, if you value security more than family, and security to you means $100,000 in the bank, you'll spend all your time making money even if it takes you away from your family. If family and relationships are most important to you, but you have to spend all of your time making money to support them, you probably won't be very happy. You might actually be happier working less and being with your family more. When you create or work in your small business, the amount of satisfaction and fulfillment you experience will be tied directly to how much that business allows you to experience your values. Knowing what you value most will help you create a business that will give you a bigger and better life.

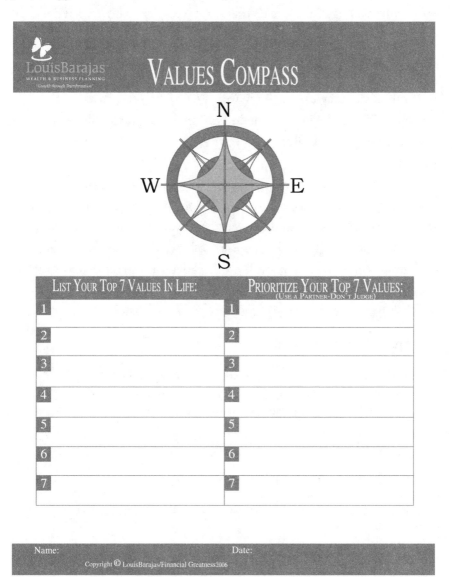

Use this form to list your top seven values. You'll discover them by asking a simple question: "What's most important to me in life?" Don't think too much; just put down what comes to your mind right away. Next to each value, jot a few words that define that value for you. For example, if "family" is your top value, define family. Is it your spouse? Your children? Your parents and/or siblings? Your closest friends? If "security" is high, what does that mean to you? An amount of money in the bank? A steady job? A certain kind of house in a good neighborhood? Your kids in good schools? A business that's running well and bringing in a specific amount of income?

While we all may use the same words ("family," "security," "happiness," "success," for instance), your definition of those words will be different from mine. Becoming clear about your values is critical to creating a life of fulfillment.

Once you have your values listed, put them in order of importance—#1 is the most important value in your life, #2 the next most important, and so on to #7. Rewrite the list in the new order. If you're so inclined, you can list more than seven values. Here is a list of my top fifteen values and the descriptions of each, to help spark your creativity as you make your own list.

LOUIS' PERSONAL VALUES

1. Spirituality (God, Faith, Hope, Love)

2. Health (Physical, Mental, Emotional, Vitality, Energy)

3. Self (Self-Care, Reflection, Introspection, Personal Growth)

4. Marriage (Intimacy)

5. Children (Unconditional Love)

6. Purpose (Meaning, Mission, Vision, Destiny, Significance)

7. Time (Balance, Priorities)

8. "Occu-passion" (Enthusiasm, Vocation, Calling, Unique Ability, Talents)

9. Financial Freedom (Choices, Options, Peace of Mind)

10. Integrity (Truth, Honesty, Character, Authenticity, Alignment)

11. Wisdom (Knowledge + Action, Discernment)

12. Contribution (Giving Back, Leaving a Legacy, Making a Difference)

13. Courage (Wisdom + Faith)

14. Self-Discipline (Self-Motivation, Burning Desire, Confidence)

15. Humility (Grounded, Sense of Humor)

I focus on these values every day. When I can experience these feelings and pay attention to these aspects of my life, I am fulfilled and happy. When you experience your own values on a daily basis, you should feel a similar sense of fulfillment.

YOUR LIFE FOCUS AREAS

To ensure that your business is part of your life and not the other way around, the next part of your life blueprint determines your major *life focus areas*. These are the different aspects of life that need your attention. For instance, if you are working hard at keeping your business going, you may not take time for exercise or regular medical check-ups. In the long term, however, you neglect the life focus area of *health* at your peril.

You may think you have a great relationship with your spouse, but spending all your time at the office year after year and failing to give your significant other the love he or she deserves will result in a less than passionate relationship at best, and a divorce at worst. To make your life work, you must be very clear about the major aspects of your life that require your time, energy, and focus. It's the only way to have both a small business and a big life.

Some life focus areas should be part of everyone's list. Your physical body is one. Relationships (with family, friends, neighbors, employees, etc.) should be one or more areas of focus. Everyone needs to focus on finances to some degree. And if you have a small business or are thinking of creating one, professional/career/business will undoubtedly be one (but *only* one) of your life focus areas. You will want to add at least one or two more areas to these four.

Using the chart on page 83, write the list of your life focus areas. After each area, write a few words describing what that area means to you.

As an illustration, here is the list of my life focus areas. Again, I don't provide these as an ideal list or even something that you should emulate. It's just an example to spark your own imagination.

Louis' Life Focus Areas

1. Physical (Body, Health, Neuro-Emotional, Fitness, Vitality, Energy)

2. Intellectual (Mind, Learning, Education, Wisdom)

3. Spiritual (Spirit, Soul, Faith, God)

4. Relational/Social (Family [marital and parental], Friends, Neighbors, Employees, Clients, Business Alliances)

5. Personal Development (Growth, Self-Care, Attractiveness, New Personal Skills)

6. Professional (Career, "Occu-passion," Calling, Work, Job)

7. Charitable (Contribution, Philanthropy, Legacy, Destiny, Cause)

8. Financial (Money, Wealth, Income, Equity)

9. Material (Purchases: Home, Auto, Clothes, Vacations, Collections)

10. Recreational (Leisure, Hobbies, Travel)

Unlike your values, you don't put your life focus areas in order of priority. Instead, you need to figure out how to balance all of these areas within your life. Once you've described your own life focus areas, give yourself a rating for the amount of time, focus, and energy you are spending in each one. On a scale of 1 to 10, 1 being lowest and 10 being highest, where do you feel you are currently in your life focus areas? Mark your current level on the form.

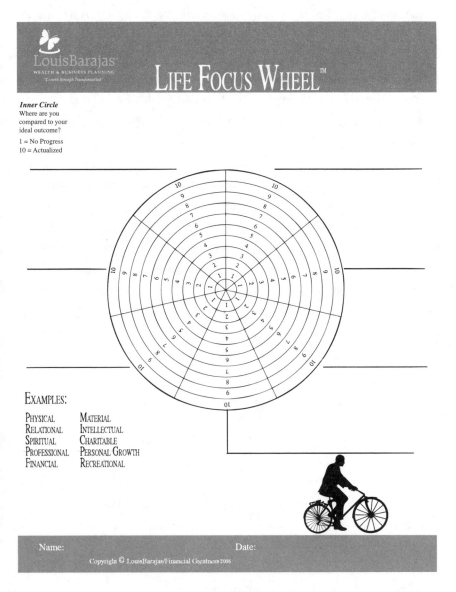

LIFE FOCUS WHEEL™

LouisBarajas
WEALTH & BUSINESS PLANNING
"Growth through Transformation"

Inner Circle
Where are you compared to your ideal outcome?

1 = No Progress
10 = Actualized

EXAMPLES:

PHYSICAL   MATERIAL
RELATIONAL   INTELLECTUAL
SPIRITUAL   CHARITABLE
PROFESSIONAL PERSONAL GROWTH
FINANCIAL   RECREATIONAL

Name: Date:

Copyright © LouisBarajas/Financial Greatness 2006

Your life focus areas are like the tires on a car: they all have to be in balance for the car to go smoothly down the road. People run into problems when they put far too much time, energy, and effort into one area and neglect all of the others. Certainly there are times in your life where you will put a lot more focus in one area. When you're starting a business, you will undoubtedly spend most of your time in the professional/career/business area. When you're in a new relationship or you have a new baby, you put more of your focus into those areas of life. But if your life is out of balance for too long, you'll start to feel dissatisfied, stressed, and unhappy. If your life currently feels out of balance, the first place to look at is your life focus areas. Ask yourself, "Where am I putting too much focus? What am I neglecting? How can I bring my life back into balance again?"

The great news is that it can take a very small amount of focus and time in any one area to bring your life back into balance. You can exercise as little as half an hour every other day and transform your body. You can spend one night a week with your spouse and transform the quality of that relationship. If you can go to one soccer game with your child each week or spend an uninterrupted afternoon with your son or daughter doing whatever he or she wants to do, you'll be astonished at the difference it will make. Decide which area or areas you want to focus on, keeping in mind that eventually you will have to put some focus on all areas to attain greatness, then put in the time to bring that area or those areas up to par.

YOUR ESSENTIAL ROLES IN LIFE

Who are you? As everyone knows, we are each many different people because we play many different roles. You may be a husband or wife or significant other; a mom or dad; a child (everyone is someone's child); a business owner (or you want to be); a citizen of planet Earth; a colleague, neighbor, friend; and on and on. Within each life focus area, we often assume a number of different roles. We experience stress when we are neglecting one or more of the important roles in our lives.

You can determine your roles in one of two ways. First, think about a typical week and ask yourself, "What roles do I fill consistently?" When you get up in the morning, are you a spouse? A parent? An athlete who runs before going to work? When you get to work, what role are you filling then? An employee? A manager? A boss? An owner? With every activity, ask, "What role is this tied to?"

Second, look at the life focus areas you just listed and ask, "What roles do I play here?" If this life focus area is one you haven't worked on in the past, perhaps you should ask yourself, "What role would I *like* to play in this life focus area?" For instance, if you need to focus more on the physical/health area, you might add "athlete" or "jock" to your list of roles. Certainly if you want to open your own small business, you want to add "business owner" to your list of professional or work roles. I have found that life focus areas become more real when we attach roles to them.

On page 87, list the roles you play, as well as those you'd like to play. Here's the list of my current roles as an example.

LOUIS' ROLES

- Husband

- Father

- Son (in-law)

- Brother (in-law)

- Uncle

- Friend

- Neighbor

- Business Owner

- Colleague

- Financial Planner

- Author/Writer

- Speaker

- Role Model (Personal)

- Mentor (Professional)

Once you identify the roles you wish to play, rate how important each role is to you. Some roles, like parent or spouse or business owner, take precedence when it comes to your time and focus. After you decide each role's importance, rate yourself on a scale of 1 to 10 (1 being lowest, 10 being highest) as to how you're fulfilling this particular role. If family and relationships are two of your life focus areas and family is high on your list of values, but you rate yourself a 4 as a parent, you may want to put some emphasis on this role by spending time with your children and becoming more actively involved in their lives.

If you want to start a small business yet you rate yourself a 3 in your current role as employee, are there challenges you're experiencing in your current job that are driving you to become an entrepreneur? Or are there parts of your current job that you don't enjoy or aren't good at? If so, will any of these tasks (administration, budgeting, time management, and so on) be important when you go out on your own? The strengths and weaknesses you can identify by analyzing your roles can help you clarify the support you will need to be successful as an entrepreneur.

While you don't need to fill in the rest of the form, there are spaces to write (1) a description of who you would be at your best in each role, (2) what's missing—what you would need to change to help you be your best—and (3) a strategy for achieving that particular result.

Using the example of a parent, if your current rating is a 4 and you want to be at least an 8, what may be missing is regular time with your children. A strategy for closing the gap might be to commit to coaching their sports team, or to make Saturday morning breakfast together a regular ritual, or perhaps to set up a mandatory family night each week when you rent DVDs or play miniature golf or do something as a family.

If you rate yourself a 5 as a potential entrepreneur, you may be missing the financial skills you feel you need to start a business. Your strategy might include taking some classes, reading books on the basics of business ownership, or perhaps hiring someone part-time to coach you on the skills you need.

ROLES GAP IDENTIFIER™

ROLE	HOW IMPORTANT IS IT?	DEFINE IDEAL OUTCOME:	WHERE ARE YOU ON THE SCALE?	WHAT'S MISSING	STRATEGY
	1 2 3 4 5 6 7 8 9 10		1 2 3 4 5 6 7 8 9 10		
	1 2 3 4 5 6 7 8 9 10		1 2 3 4 5 6 7 8 9 10		
	1 2 3 4 5 6 7 8 9 10		1 2 3 4 5 6 7 8 9 10		
	1 2 3 4 5 6 7 8 9 10		1 2 3 4 5 6 7 8 9 10		
	1 2 3 4 5 6 7 8 9 10		1 2 3 4 5 6 7 8 9 10		
	1 2 3 4 5 6 7 8 9 10		1 2 3 4 5 6 7 8 9 10		

Name: _____ Date: _____

Copyright © LouisBarajas/Financial Greatness 2006

Knowing the roles you play on a daily basis will make it easier to be effective and efficient in creating a fulfilling life. It also will help you create better relationships and maintain a sense of balance even when you're pushing hard to get your business started or to develop your company.

If you have been reading this book without doing the exercises in this chapter, stop now and go back and do them! The return on your investment of time, thought, and energy will be significant.

USING YOUR LIFE BLUEPRINT
TO DESIGN THE LIFE OF YOUR DREAMS

Let's say you and I were flying from Orange County, California, (where I live) to Atlanta, Georgia. When you board most transcontinental flights, what do you see? The first four to six rows are first class, with big seats and lots of legroom. The next several rows are business class. The seats are smaller than first class but still pretty cushy. In both first class and business class you get complimentary wine and liquor, dishes of mixed nuts, hot towels, and meals throughout the flight.

If you can't afford first class or business class, where do you go? Economy class. The seats are cramped, and maybe you get pretzels and soda pop—but no mixed nuts, no meals, and no hot towels. There also is an even lower level of transport on the plane. If you didn't need to make the trip yourself but wanted to send your dog for some reason, your pet would ride in the cargo hold. Here's the point: whether we ride in first class, business class, coach, or the cargo hold, all of us on the plane are going to the same destination. We all arrive at the same place; it's just that some of us will travel in greater comfort.

Our lives are like that. We're all on the same journey; the question is, how do you want to travel? In the case of your life, how you travel has something to do with how much you pay for the "ticket," but it has a lot more to do with what you decide is most important when it comes to living every day.

The unfortunate thing is that most of us are on the airplane with absolutely no idea of what would make the journey a first-class one for us. There's nothing sadder than people who reach the end of their journey filled with regrets over the choices they've made—or worse, having gone through life letting life dictate their choices instead of choosing for themselves.

Your life blueprint is a map of the journey of your life. It can show you clearly where you are succeeding and where you need to put more focus. It will tell you exactly what you need to do, be, and have for your life to be completely "first class." You will use your life blueprint to help you set goals for every life focus area, based on what you believe is most important to you (your values) and the roles you feel you must fulfill in order to be truly happy.

Once my clients have created their life blueprints, I suggest that they spend a couple of hours creating the *goals* that will give them the greatest satisfaction. What are their goals for their physical health? Their relationships? Their finances? Their spiritual goals? The contributions they want to make? And how will accomplishing those goals give them more of the emotions they value? How will these goals make them better parents, spouses, employers, teachers—whatever they consider their key roles? When your goals are linked to your values, roles, and life focus areas, you will experience more fulfillment, both while you pursue those goals and when you attain them.

Your life blueprint also will help you plan ways to make your small business fit into the rest of your life. All my clients check their life blueprints frequently, whenever they create goals for their business. By using the life blueprint as a checklist, you can ensure that the efforts you are putting into your business will give you more satisfaction and fulfillment instead of fatigue and frustration.

Let me give you a hypothetical example. My client, Joe, comes to me and says, "Louis, I want to open another store. I have the money ready and I've found the perfect spot. I'd like to open my doors in a month. Look at all the money I'll make!"

The first thing I suggest to Joe is to check his plans against his life blueprint and the goals he has for himself in the other areas of his life. "You told me at the beginning of the year that your son is going off to college in September," I remind him. "Do you have all the financing for his schooling in place? How is opening another store this spring going to affect the cash you'll need for that?"

"If the store does as well as I think it will, it should mean I have more money," Joe says to me with a wave of his hand.

"But what if it doesn't? As you know, most new ventures require more investment than you're planning for. Are you willing to put off your son going to college if your store needs more capital?"

Joe shakes his head. "Absolutely not—my son's not waiting to go to school. This is a big step for him, and he's worked too hard to wait."

"Alright, then, how could you make sure to have the capital to send your son to school and still open another store?"

"Well . . ." Joe thinks a moment. "I could either postpone opening a new store until next year and put the money I've been setting aside into my son's college account instead. Or I could find an outside investor to put up half of the money. Or I could talk with my banker and see about getting a bigger loan so I'd have to put up less of the initial capital for equipment and marketing. It would mean I'd make less from the store in the first couple of years, but my son would be guaranteed a college education, and that means more to me than a bigger bank account."

Checking your business goals against your life blueprint means you keep your focus on what's truly important to you. It allows your business to be part of your life rather than having to fit your life into your business. Ultimately, I believe it makes it easier to achieve your goals because you have eliminated potential conflicts that might prevent you from going after what you want wholeheartedly.

YOUR GUIDE TO A MORE BALANCED LIFE

Using your life blueprint as your guide to creating a business and life also will give you more balance and ultimately more happiness. How many business owners have dropped dead of heart attacks or found themselves divorced or alone, because they poured everything into their work? There's nothing more draining than having to play catch-up in an important area or role because you've neglected it. It's like physical exercise: it's easier to maintain a certain level of fitness once you've achieved it than to get there in the first place. I've seen far too many clients who let their health slide and their relationships weaken because they've spent too much time on their businesses.

I've also known others who weren't putting enough time and energy into the different roles they needed to fill as a business owner, and as a result their businesses were in trouble. That's why I spend a lot of time with clients helping them develop a clear understanding of their life blueprints so that they can experience greater success and fulfillment in all areas of life. I tell them, "Let's talk about your values, your roles, and your life focus areas. Let's see how to build a great life, and then we can talk about building a business to give you the life of your dreams."

All entrepreneurs face the risk that their business will take over their lives. But when it comes to the end of your life, do you want to look back and say, "I was so successful in my business that I neglected my family, alienated my spouse, destroyed my health, and never enjoyed anything other than a great bottom line"?

There's a very well-known character in literature who lived his life in exactly that way: Ebenezer Scrooge. Scrooge lived only for his business and was famous for being a tightfisted, crotchety miser—until three spirits showed him the consequences of his ways. To ensure that your business is *part* of your life rather than being *all* of your life, you must design your life blueprint first. With your life blueprint as a guide, and using what you will learn in the next few chapters, you can create both the successful business and the fulfilled and happy life you've always wanted.

7

STEP 2: Your Vision

The Source of Leadership

Whether your small business is just you alone or you have one hundred employees, if it's your business, you are the leader. You cannot *not* be the leader—you are responsible for the direction of the business, the day-to-day decision making, the workplace atmosphere, and on and on. The leadership of your business must begin and end with you.

The same cornerstones we spoke of in part 1—truth, responsibility, awareness, and courage—form the foundation of all great leadership. You start by telling the *truth* about yourself and your business. People must feel they can trust you as their leader, and trust is born of honesty. Think of some of the leaders in our country—political figures like Nixon and Clinton, industry leaders like Kenneth Lay of Enron—who have lied. How much damage did their lies do to their ability to lead?

You also have to take *responsibility*. There's a saying that with leadership comes responsibility—well, with responsibility comes leadership. You have to believe "the buck stops here" and take care of what needs to be done.

As a leader, you must be *aware* of the needs of your people, your company, your industry, and your community. And last, you must have *courage.* Most people know what they need to do but don't have the courage to do it. You have to be willing to say, "This is what we will do," and take others along with you in the direction you have chosen.

On this foundation, you can build your ground floor based on the leadership trait of *vision.* The purpose of a leader in a business environment is to create the vision for the business. Vision creates direction and confidence. Vision takes you from the present moment and connects you to a better future. As an entrepreneur, you must develop a clear vision of your business before you ever hire anyone or deposit your first check. You must have confidence in your vision, take responsibility for creating it, and have the courage to continue on the path even when the odds are against success.

Three thousand years ago King Solomon said, "Where there is no vision, the people perish" (Proverbs 29:18 KJV). I have seen this lack of vision in the barrio where I grew up. In 2005, Garfield High School in East Los Angeles had more than a 50 percent dropout rate (and that number doesn't include all the kids who drop out before they reach high school). Despite a lot of attention and funding and initiatives like "No Child Left Behind," the dropout rate at Garfield has been just about the same for the last ten to twenty years.

Why? I believe that one of the reasons is a lack of vision. Parents are so focused on making ends meet that all they can deal with is the present. Kids drop out because they think, *It never got better for my parents, it won't get better for me, so why should I stay in school?* They don't realize that the way to make their lives different starts by creating a *vision* of something better.

I was fortunate that my dad and mom had a vision of things being different for our family. My father worked extremely hard, but more important, he encouraged me to think that I could do whatever I wanted. With the leadership and vision of people like my dad, I and many others like me have created very different lives for ourselves. And we owe it to those who have held their vision in the face of adversity and shared the importance of vision with the next generation of entrepreneurs—like you.

DOUBLE VISION

I believe that as a small business owner you need a kind of double vision. First, you must have a vision for your life *and* a vision for your business. As we said in the last chapter, the vision for your business must be compatible with, and a part of, your life blueprint. When you create the vision for your business, you should always ask, "How does this fit into my life blueprint, which is my ultimate vision for who I am and how I want to live?"

Second, small business owners need double vision in order to pay attention to both the present and the future. The vision for your business must include the present (current situation) and the future (what the business will look like when it is up and running, or when you retire or sell). Like your life blueprint, your vision for your business must begin with the end in mind. Far too many business owners get caught up in the day-to-day routine of making payroll, satisfying customers, and getting the product out the door. They fail to keep their eyes on the "prize" of a business that runs smoothly, creates consistent and expanding value, and builds equity so they can sell the business at a profit or pass along a valuable asset to their heirs.

Chapter 1 presented the differences among being an employee, a manager, a self-employed person, and a business owner. When you start your own business, you hear over and over again that you have to work hard, put your nose to the grindstone and your shoulder to the wheel, and work 24/7 until your business is up and running. But that's the mind-set of the self-employed person. If you're going to make the transition from self-employed to business owner, you can't get caught up in focusing only on the needs of today or next week. You have to have one eye on the present and the other on the future. You can't get caught up in today at the expense of planning for tomorrow.

I saw this problem not too long ago when I got a call from a young woman in Florida. She was twenty-three years old, from Colombia, and owned a custom closet business with her brothers. "We're all three working really hard, but we're not making any money," she told me.

"What do you think the problem is?" I asked.

"We can't seem to find the right kind of clients," she answered.

"Well then, tell me about your marketing plan. What are you doing to help clients come to you?" I said. (We call this *customer attraction.*)

"We don't have a marketing plan," she said.

"What about your closing ratio? Do you know how many clients you close? What's your satisfaction and referral rate?" (This is *strategic thinking*—thinking about what you're doing rather than simply doing more of what you're currently doing.)

"We're just too busy to think about that kind of stuff," she protested.

"Then you're just too busy, period," I told her. "Because the stuff that you're not thinking about is what's going to create success in your business."

If you are going to make the transition to business owner, you have to create your vision and then take the time to do the strategic planning that will get you there. For new business owners, this is particularly difficult. They usually don't have the resources to be able to get someone to run the business while they plan. They have to work on their business every day no matter what. But the time you take to create your vision is the most important time you can spend.

Someone once said that thinking is very hard work, and that's why so few people do it. Creating a vision is also very hard work—that's why so few people do it and why so few small businesses are successful. Without a vision, people perish. Without a future-based vision, your business is in danger of perishing as well.

YOUR VISION OF THE IDEAL BUSINESS

Deciding on the vision for your business can even help you decide what business to start. If you're already in business, it can help you assess what you're doing in order to make it more enjoyable, or it can help you make the decision to do something else. When your vision for your business matches the reality of what you are doing, you have a recipe for success and fulfillment for both a small business and a big life.

Let's assume you're just starting your business. Many people choose a business based on one of two factors: *necessity* or *training/background*. As we discussed in chapter 1, some people start a business out of necessity, to make enough money to support themselves and their families. Common examples of necessity-based businesses include selling oranges on freeway on-ramps, hawking blue blocker sunglasses at flea markets, and holding garage sales every weekend. A lot of people go into multilevel marketing out of necessity. They're working full-time already, and they see or hear the ads about making thousands in your spare time. None of these businesses require much capital or talent, and they certainly require little or no personal vision. Unfortunately, these "businesses" are more like self-employment, and their future is very limited.

The second factor in choosing a business is training or background. Take my father, for example. He had worked at a big lighting manufacturing company for several years, so when he decided to go out on his own, he first opened a lighting manufacturing company in a commercial space about three blocks from where we lived. However, Dad's business didn't do all that well, so he rented out part of his shop to a man who did ornamental ironwork. Because things were slow in the lighting business and the ornamental ironwork man was doing well, my dad would help him out working with the iron. Dad found he really enjoyed it, so when the ornamental iron man got into legal troubles and offered to sell my father the business, Dad jumped at the chance.

People like my dad take a talent or hobby or something they've been trained to do and try to turn it into a successful business. This may be more successful than just starting any old business—at least these people have a shot at producing a product or service that people will actually buy. But to turn a hobby or talent into a true business requires a great deal of vision, preparation, and work. And you must have a vision for all aspects of the business because all aspects of the business must work together. Like the young woman in Florida, it's not enough to build great closets if you don't have a way to contact the right clients and if you don't have systems to close the sale and get referrals.

THE THREE COMPONENTS
OF A SUCCESSFUL VISION

Instead of choosing a business simply out of necessity or based on a particular talent or training, I believe that the vision for your business must be based on something that Jim Collins describes in his book *Good to Great.* Collins talks about a great business occurring when three different things intersect: (1) something you love to do, (2) something you're great at doing, and (3) something that makes a profit. The following diagram illustrates these factors.

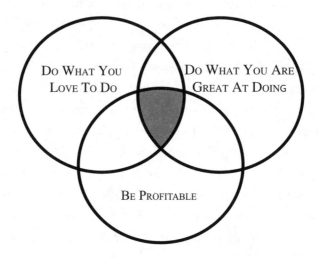

1. DO WHAT YOU LOVE TO DO

What would you do if you could choose any business in the world? No matter how much money a business has the potential to make, unless you love what the business does, you're not likely to make a go of it. On the other hand, when you find a business that is tied to something that you'd do even if nobody paid you to do it, then you've found something that will get you up in the morning and keep you working for the long hours it usually takes to get a business started. To be successful in the long run, I believe that your business must be something you love to do—what I call your "occu-passion."

Think about people who have started small businesses and turned them into big ones. Bill Gates. Steve Jobs. Larry Page and Sergey Brin, the founders of Google. Michael Dell. Warren Buffett. Martha Stewart. Richard Branson of Virgin Airlines. Mary Kay Ash. Fred Smith of Federal Express. Walt Disney. They were truly passionate about their businesses. They loved what they did so much that they put in the time and energy to turn their small companies into household names. Even if you don't have that kind of ambition, having a vision for a business that allows you to do what you love is critical for long-term success.

2. Do What You Are Great at Doing

Your vision for your business also should be based upon your unique ability—in Spanish, we call it *tu don,* your God-given gift. I'm not just talking about your product or service; you have to be good at what the business is at its core. If you're not good at talking to people, for example, a multi-level marketing business probably isn't going to be your cup of tea even if you adore the product. If you're a great cook but you hate managing people, you will have a lot of trouble should you decide to open a restaurant (unless you have a partner who will handle that aspect of the business for you).

Let me use myself as an example. I went into finance because I'm good with numbers, but my real gift is communicating with people. When I went with my dad on sales calls and translated for him, he would tell me, "You have a gift, a *don,* for communicating and helping people. You have to protect your gift."

I love helping people improve their finances and businesses. I'm really passionate about it. I'm also good at taking complicated subjects and talking about them in such a way that people will understand. When I was doing taxes for people, my business was good, but it really took off when I was able to use my *don,* my God-given talent, by teaching seminars, writing financial columns, and eventually writing a book on financial greatness and speaking about it all over the country.

When I went to college, however, I thought my gift lay in another direction. I'd graduated from high school a semester early and went to a training program that taught marketable skills. The business section of the program was full, so I signed up for medical training. I became a licensed medical assistant; in fact, my job that summer was working for an osteopath, giving shots and running tests. So when I went to UCLA, I thought I'd go into pre-med classes.

But I did horribly. I studied nonstop, but I still almost failed several classes. "I don't think this is my *don,* my gift," I said to myself. I transferred out of premed and eventually graduated with honors in my chosen major, sociology. From there I went on to get my MBA. Today I feel I'm using my *don* in my current business.

People as diverse as Diana Kennedy (who is an incredible cook of Mexican cuisine and has written many cookbooks), Martha Stewart (who parlayed her home decorating and crafts expertise into a decorating and media empire), and Howard Schultz (who loved coffee) of Starbucks have turned their *dons* into successful businesses. All of us have some God-given ability. The question is how to turn yours into something that can be a profitable business.

3. BE PROFITABLE

That's the third element of a successful business: it must be profitable! Otherwise, you don't have a business: you have a hobby. I see so many people who have a multilevel marketing business, and they're very happy with it. They love what they're doing; they're great at talking about the product and enrolling others in the business. But they're not focused on being profitable. I'm certainly not against multilevel marketing as long as people are clear on the fact that, in most cases, what they have is more accurately called a hobby that pays for itself rather than a profit-producing business. Until you treat your multilevel marketing business as just that—a business—you won't be able to take advantage of the success it can offer.

As Michael Gerber writes in *The E-Myth Revisited,* "Just because you know how to do something doesn't mean you know how to run a business that does that thing." Developing your business requires profit. Paying talented employees requires profit. Obtaining quality support, quality materials, and so on requires profit.

Far too many business owners go into business "to make money" from their talents, but then they forget the profit motivation along the way. While profit shouldn't be your only motivation, it is equal to the other two factors of loving what you do and being good at the core aspect of your business.

If you look at the diagram on page 98 you'll notice there's a "sweet spot" where all three circles intersect. This is the spot where you love what you do, you're good at it, and you can make money in a business that does that same thing. In this spot, you can look beyond yourself and your business and start focusing on giving to others, making a difference, and creating a legacy that will outlive both you and your business.

Think about people like Warren Buffett, Bill Gates, Andrew Carnegie, and John D. Rockefeller. When they found their passion and created businesses that did well, they naturally focused on giving back some of the gifts that had been given to them. I believe that all of us can reach that same point of entrepreneurial greatness.

FIVE VISION QUESTIONS

Let's spend some time discovering the vision for your business. You can do this process whether you have a business already or you wish to start one now or in the future. Please take the time to think about the following questions and answer them fully, in writing.

QUESTION 1. WHAT IS YOUR "OCCU-PASSION"?

What are the things you love to do? You can include hobbies, interests, parts of your current job you enjoy, and parts of other jobs that you think you'd really like. Try to make this list as wide-ranging as you can. You never know what could lead to a profitable business—people can make money coaching soccer, owning a scrapbook franchise, using gardening or cooking skills, leading tour groups as they travel around the world, or any number of activities that might be considered hobbies or sports.

Another way to think of your "occu-passion" is to remember occasions when time seemed to fly by because you were so engrossed in what you were doing. If there are parts of your current job when that happens, write those down as well. Some people get engrossed in building something, designing something, writing, teaching, or coaching, that they lose all track of time. Whatever that is for you, write it down. The goal is to develop a big list of everything you really love to do.

QUESTION 2. WHAT ARE YOU GREAT AT? WHAT IS YOUR UNIQUE GIFT?

Everyone has talents. What are yours? What have people said you excel at doing? What have you received recognition for? What parts of your current job or business do you find really easy? Are you great with numbers? A great writer? A great speaker? A great coach? A great negotiator? Great with computers? A whiz at figuring out machines? An artist or craftsperson or designer?

Again, write down everything at which you excel, and for everything you write, make sure to ask yourself, "What skill or ability makes me great at this?" You may find that organizing is one of your talents, or managing or coaching others, or bringing people to consensus, or getting the job done quickly. You might be a great salesperson or great at detail or really good at verbalizing the big picture. You could be an inspiring speaker or leader. You could be a great team player.

Remember to include hobbies and other areas of your life when taking a look at your abilities. Someone who's a great parent could also be great at running a day care center. Someone who's a superb singer in a church choir could coach other singers, help with the music for a group, or even write and arrange choral music. Again, your goal is to capture everything you feel you're great at.

Often your gift is something that comes so easily to you that you don't see it as a gift. "I'm just naturally good with numbers!" you might say. Or

"Sure, it's easy for me to decorate my house or arrange flowers. What's the big deal?" One way to discover your gift is to ask others. I have clients write letters to ten colleagues and friends, asking, "If you could name one thing I'm great at, what would it be?" Usually there's a consensus that emerges from the responses.

Like Tiger Woods, Michael Jordan, Martha Stewart, Madonna, and the winners of *American Idol*, you have certain unique and special gifts. You just need to discover them and put them to use in your business.

QUESTION 3. HOW COULD THE ANSWERS TO QUESTIONS 1 AND 2 BE TURNED INTO A PROFITABLE BUSINESS?

Let your imagination run wild in this question! You'll have plenty of time to get very practical later. Right now, take a look at your answers to questions 1 and 2 and write down absolutely every kind of business that could possibly utilize your passion and your gifts. Could you run a sports team? Open a restaurant? Sell your artwork? Design beautiful gardens? Fix classic cars? Teach kids? Write a book? Train athletes? Become a professional negotiator? List every possible way you could turn your passion and your talents into a profitable business.

QUESTION 4. WHAT THREE CHOICES ENGAGE YOUR PASSION, UTILIZE YOUR GIFTS, AND MAKE A PROFIT?

Look at your list and circle your top three choices for a business. Make sure you take into account the life blueprint you created in the last chapter so you can fit your business into your life rather than the other way around. The key here is not to eliminate businesses because of "practical" reasons ("I'll never get the capital to open a high-end jewelry store") but to choose the top three businesses that engage your passion, utilize your talents, and stand a chance of producing a fair amount of profit.

QUESTION 5. WHAT IS MY VISION FOR THIS BUSINESS?

Now you can start working on a vision for the business that will help you create the life of your dreams. Take any one of your top three choices and start by imagining a typical day in the first year of that business. What would you be doing? What product or service would you be producing? Who are your customers? How many hours will you work? Where will your business be? How many employees will you have? What will your receipts be? Which parts of your day do you love, and are there other parts you're working on delegating? How is your business reflecting your passion and your gifts?

Next, take that vision five years in the future. What's your business like now? How has it grown? How many employees do you have? How many customers per year? What have you done to expand? How are you enjoying the work you're doing now? What have you successfully delegated? What more have you taken on once your time was freed up? What difference are you able to make in the lives of your employees and the community? How great does it feel to walk into your business and say, "I created this"? How have you grown in the course of building your business? What have you learned? How much more are you utilizing your "occu-passion" and your *don*?

TURNING VISION INTO REALITY TAKES A PLAN

Once you've created your vision, you're ready to make it a reality. The rest of this section will give you the tools you need to create a business blueprint, put in place the systems you need to make your business successful, and gather and inspire the team that will help you take your business from small to great. In appendix A, you'll find a goal-setting system that will help you turn your vision into a reality.

Usually we think of leadership as standing in front of a group and saying, "This is what we will do. Let's march!" But true leadership starts within. You must create a vision inside your own mind with lots of thought, preparation, and dreaming before you can enroll yourself and others in making that vision a reality. If you lead yourself into creating a vision for your business, you'll find that creating that vision in the outside world will be easier than you could ever dream.

8

STEP 3: Your Business Blueprint

Your Business Is Your Business, *Not Your Product or Service.*

I magine that my wife, Angie, and I are in a strange city and we want to go out to dinner. We're not sure where to go, but there are a lot of restaurants close to our hotel. I'm craving Mexican food, so we ask the concierge at our hotel if there's a Mexican restaurant close by. He looks in the *Yellow Pages* and finds one within a mile or so.

We get in our rental car and drive toward the restaurant's address. We see a Chinese restaurant on one corner, a Denny's across the street, and a couple of nice-looking steak and seafood places. But when we get to the street address of the Mexican restaurant, it's hard to spot. There's no lighting on the sign, and the stores in the same block look like they all closed at around five o'clock. We're going to have to park on the street because there's no parking lot.

"Are you sure we want to eat here?" my wife asks. Despite my misgivings, I really want some Mexican food, and so I drop her off and park the car a couple of blocks away. I walk back to the restaurant, go inside, and find Angie still waiting for a table even though the place is not completely full.

"Where's the host or hostess?" I ask.

"I haven't seen anyone yet," she says. "One of the waiters told me someone would be with us in a minute, but it's been five minutes already."

Fifteen minutes later, we're just about to walk out the door and find another restaurant when someone comes bustling in from the back. "Sorry, sorry, have you been waiting long? Let me get you a table," she says. She looks around, yells to the busboy, "Hurry up and clean table five!" and then says to us, "Give us one more minute—we just finished serving a very large party and we're kind of backed up."

That's no excuse, I think. But we're here and we've already waited almost half an hour, so what's one more minute? Indeed, we're seated just as soon as the table's cleared, we have our menus and water glasses—and it's another ten minutes before the waiter comes to take our order. I'm starting to feel guilty for making my wife wait this long for dinner. I flag a waiter passing by and ask, "Excuse me, can you get our waiter?"

"I *am* your waiter," he answers. He takes out his order pad and says, "Okay, what do you want to drink?"

We get our drink orders pretty quickly (thank goodness), but when the entrée comes, the waiter serves me first. It's really good food, but Angie's meal doesn't arrive until ten minutes later. Now, I'm a fast eater, so I have almost finished before Angie has gotten her meal.

When the bill comes, I find a small error, so I have to get the waiter, show it to him, and wait for a revised bill. Even though the food was good, when I go back to the hotel I make a point of telling the concierge about our bad experience.

Have you ever talked to business owners and asked them what they do for a living? One hundred percent of the time they will describe the product that they make or the service that they provide. But you can make the greatest Mexican food in town, and if your restaurant isn't well located and well lit, if your servers don't take care of the customers, and if you spend too much and charge too little, you're in trouble.

Just because you know how to do something that doesn't mean you know how to run a business that does that something. You can have the greatest product or service in the world, but unless you have created a *business* to support that product or service, your small business is not going to be around for very long.

E-Myth author Michael Gerber is famous for saying, "The business of your business is your business." Most new entrepreneurs rarely have a clue as to all the tasks that are required to run a business on a day-to-day basis. It's like someone coming to you and saying, "Please build me a car." Now, you may be aware of the different pieces that go into a car—wheels, an engine, a muffler, a body, and so on—but unless you've studied auto mechanics, you wouldn't have much of an idea of how they all fit together. You'd be standing next to a big pile of auto parts saying, "Is this the transmission? Is this part of the exhaust? Exactly where do the spark plugs go? Is this the front or rear axle?"

That's how a lot of potential entrepreneurs approach their businesses. They know they need to have a product or service, they know they need customers, and they know they need systems to deliver the product or service, to get paid, and to pay for materials and supplies. *How* to do all of that, however, is not something they've ever done or studied. The rest of part 2 is designed to teach you how to assemble the "car" that is your small business so that it will run well and carry you to a profitable and successful future.

CREATING YOUR BUSINESS BLUEPRINT

Most would-be entrepreneurs know they need to put together a business plan, and they find information on creating one. A business plan describes your product or service and lays out your projected revenues, expenses, start-up costs, capital needed to begin, and more. The main purpose of a business plan is to get funding from a bank or other financial backers. In my nearly twenty years of experience working with business owners, 95 out of 100 business owners never have a business plan, and if they put one together in the initial stages, it's only because they were seeking a Small Business Administration loan or some other type of financing.

Most business plans are very cursory—the owners talk about who their competitors are, what the market is like, and why they need the money. This kind of plan is not a guide for running a business; it's just a means of proving to lenders that the business is a good risk. However, once you have the money, how do you know what to do with it?

That's where a *business blueprint* comes in. A business blueprint clearly identifies all the major functions and tasks that are required to run your business. In the same way that your life blueprint shows you how to have a successful and fulfilling life, a business blueprint will make it possible for you to have a successful and fulfilling business.

Every small business has three goals:

(1) to attract, satisfy, and retain customers,

(2) to create and manage cash flow, and

(3) to support the team that will help your business grow.

Think of those goals as the destination. Your small business is the vehicle—the car—that will get you there. But for the vehicle to make it from point A to point B, it has to fulfill several functions. The fuel in the car has to burn. The engine needs to be kept at a certain temperature. The wheels have to stay on the road and keep turning. The accelerator and brakes have to work. When all these functions are working well, your vehicle will go smoothly and swiftly to your destination.

Your business blueprint describes the functions your business must fulfill for it to run smoothly and well. On page 109 you'll see a simplified version of a business blueprint.

A lot of big businesses have organizational charts that show the different divisions or departments of a company and describe who reports to whom. A business blueprint is different because it shows the different *functions* your business needs to fulfill on a daily basis. With a business blueprint, you can have one person handle many functions (as happens in

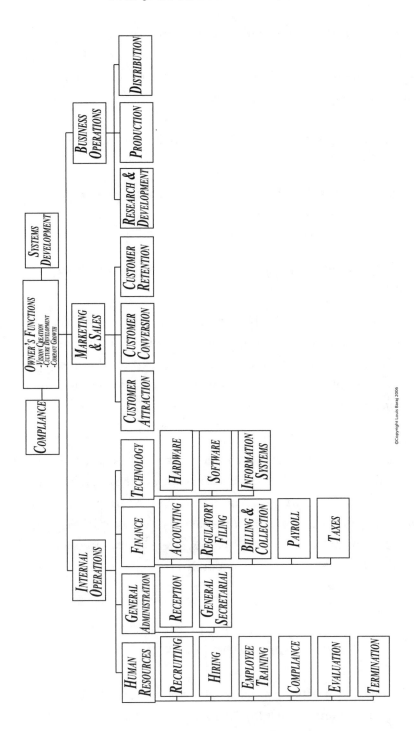

©Copyright Louis Baraj 2006

most small businesses), but you also can ensure that someone is handling all the functions, even if that "someone" is you, the owner. This blueprint shows the general categories of functions that need to be handled in any business. There are four key functions.

1. *The owner's responsibilities.* These are things that you as the owner must handle.

2. *Internal operations.* This includes everything it takes to run the business "backstage," so to speak—all of the human resource functions, finances, technology, etc.

3. *Marketing and sales.* This encompasses everything you do to find, attract, sell, and retain customers.

4. *Business operations.* This is the part of your business that actually produces and delivers your product or service. But while most entrepreneurs consider it the most critical part of a business, in truth it's only of equal (or perhaps even less) importance to the other three.

In this chapter we're going to talk about each of these categories so you can get a grasp on exactly what the business of your business will require. Whether you're just starting out or already have a business with several employees, these categories must form part of your business blueprint. (In the next chapter, "Your Business Systems," we will discuss how to make each of these functions run most smoothly.)

THE FIRST KEY FUNCTION:
THE OWNER'S RESPONSIBILITIES

On the business blueprint on page 109, you see three functions at the very top. These are *compliance, "big picture" thinking* (which includes vision creation, culture development, and company growth), and *systems development*. Let's go over the components of each.

1. COMPLIANCE

Remember we said in chapter 7 that the buck has to stop with the business owner? Ultimately you're responsible for ensuring that your business complies with all existing legal requirements. You must keep your business license current. You must pay your taxes on time. You must file the required forms for your employees. You must follow all local, state, and federal workplace regulations. You must make sure you have the necessary insurance to operate your business, and then you must make sure your workplace and employees comply with the requirements of that insurance. None of this is enjoyable, but if you want to stay in business, you'd better take responsibility for all compliance issues. As we've seen in companies like Enron, "I didn't know" or "they didn't tell me" is not an adequate legal defense.

2. "BIG PICTURE" THINKING

As the owner, you're responsible for the "big picture"—the vision that guides the business, the culture creation that maintains it, and the growth planning to ensure it will be viable for the long term. You cannot or should not delegate these three responsibilities because they provide some of the key drivers of your business. They are what will truly make a business yours, an expression of your unique abilities, passions, and dreams.

Vision

As we said in the last chapter, one of the main functions of the owner is to consistently create, hold, and update the vision for the company. You, and only you, can create the big picture of your business. Your vision and dreams, coupled with strategies, actions, and, above all, systems, will dictate its direction.

If you have a partner or partners, you should realize that there usually can be only one visionary in any company. Multiple visions create conflict. I saw this happen in my first business. As I built the business, my vision changed somewhat. I had started the company to provide financial services to the underserved, and after a few years I expanded the vision to include more education, business planning, and consulting.

However, my partner's vision was to build a business focused on accounting and bookkeeping. I was doing a lot of outreach, teaching, writing, and speaking; he was more comfortable simply providing accounting services. Our employees were getting mixed messages about what they should be doing and where they should put their focus.

Eventually I decided to leave and start my own company that would allow me to do the kind of consulting and outreach that is my true "occu-passion." My current business is built on my vision of creating a financial revolution for the working class. Everyone who works with me is included in that vision, and we're all working toward the same goal.

Having competing visions is like being in a boat with two rowers pulling in opposite directions. All you do is go in circles, while exhausting both you and the other person. I've worked with hundreds of small businesses that have more than one owner and no vision or designated visionary, and these businesses usually don't survive. If your business has more than one owner, you need to make sure that all partners share the same vision.

Culture Development

Have you ever walked into someone's home and felt either comfortable or uncomfortable? There's a certain atmosphere, a culture, about the home that you like or dislike. It's the same for your business. Banks have one type of culture; sports stores have another. The culture you create will determine the type of employees and clients you will attract.

What type of culture do you want to create in your business? Do you want to create a company that works hard and plays hard? Do you want to create a company that supports the growth of its employees or one that is focused on competition and backstabbing? Like your vision for the company, culture is something you must create actively and revisit continually to make sure it represents the kind of place in which you and your employees are proud to work.

Company Growth

There was a great commercial on television a few years ago. A Web site business was just getting ready to go online. All the employees gathered around a computer screen and cheered as the first orders came in from the Web site. Then their faces fell as hundreds, then thousands, and then millions of orders came pouring in. You could tell they weren't ready to handle that many orders. One of the employees turned to the others and said, "We're in real trouble, aren't we?"

Growing too slowly is obviously not good for you, but growing too fast is one of the main causes of business bankruptcy. As the owner of your company, you will have to keep an eye on growth. You will need to review how much work or clients you can handle and then plan for an orderly expansion so that you can provide the best products or services in the most cost efficient ways. If you are starting a business, before you ever open your doors you need to plan for growth.

3. SYSTEMS DEVELOPMENT

As the owner, you must look consistently for any problem or frustration in your company and try to develop a system to cure it. For example, if you have a recurring problem with different employees, the problem is not with the employees but with the system (or lack of system) of recruiting, training, evaluating, and rewarding. As you'll hear time and again in chapter 9, the system is the solution.

THE SECOND KEY FUNCTION:
INTERNAL OPERATIONS

These are all the nonsexy jobs of a company. Think of it as the pipes for the plumbing in your house. The pipes may not be particularly pretty, but if one of them breaks or even gets clogged, your bathtub or kitchen sink or toilet or dishwasher or washing machine will cease to function, causing no end of trouble. In the same way, your customers probably will never see your company's internal operations, but they will see the results of problems with your employees or your billing or your computers or your telephones.

When you start your business, you as the owner probably will have to handle or oversee all of the internal operations of your business. I would suggest one of two things. First, if you're going to be the one responsible for internal operations, do your best to educate yourself so you can make the fewest mistakes. Your goal is to get to the point where you have a basic familiarity with most internal operations. Something as simple as being able to operate the fax machine or to update your Web site yourself can make the difference between staying in business and shutting down for a day while you wait for a technician to arrive.

Second, as soon as possible, see if you can hire an outside service for some of these internal operations. Many excellent services are available to handle human resources, billing, Web site maintenance, and other internal operations. Using an outside expert rather than trying to do it all yourself will enable you to focus on more important tasks—like creating the vision, attracting clients, and providing the best product or service.

There are four basic areas of internal operations: human resources, general administration, finance, and technology.

1. HUMAN RESOURCES
This includes everything having to do with employees and the rules and regulations that concern employment: recruiting, hiring, benefits, training, workplace rules compliance, evaluation, termination, dispute settlement,

and so on. Things like workers' compensation, workplace injury, sexual harassment, discrimination, and other "hot button" areas fall in this category. You can see why most companies with seventy-five or more employees hire a full-time human resource manager! A good human resource manager will cost $50,000 a year and more in annual salary. For most startup businesses (as well as the 90 percent of all companies in the United States that have fewer than twenty-five employees), that's too expensive. However, you should consider using a human resource *consultant* as soon as you hire your very first employee. At the very least, find some good, comprehensive guides and read about your obligations as an employer.

2. GENERAL ADMINISTRATION

This includes all the administrative tasks that need to be done on a daily basis, such as answering phones, greeting clients, delivering messages, distributing mail, typing letters, ordering office supplies, and handling general client customer service. Remember the story of my first year in business? I only made $12,000, but I got to the point where I couldn't spend time with clients because I was always answering the phone. So I hired an administrative assistant to help me, and the next year I not only paid her salary but doubled my own income as well. Getting administrative help can be relatively inexpensive, and if it frees you up to see more clients, create more product, or work on expanding your business, it's some of the best money you can spend.

3. FINANCE

This includes accounting, billing, payments, collections, payroll, taxes, and government regulations compliance. Most small business owners start by doing their own bookkeeping and then hire an accountant to file any necessary paperwork. They may also hire a company to do the payroll and file all necessary regulatory documents. In my experience in working with small business owners, however, these financial functions are some of the most, if not *the* most, neglected areas of business—even though failing to keep close track of where your money is coming from and where it's going would seem to be one of the dumbest things an owner can do!

Sometimes small business owners fail to set up adequate financial systems for shady reasons. Local banks send me a lot of potential clients— people who are trying to get loans to expand their mom-and-pop businesses. The bankers tell me, "Louis, we know the company is making money. We know this client owns his own house, and we know that he's doing well personally. But the company financial statements don't show us anything. They may be doing a lot of cash business and not putting it on the books, or their bookkeepers are not doing a good job, or maybe they're trying to keep their receipts low to save on taxes. But because their income isn't showing up on their financial statements, we can't loan them any money."

People like this are in a catch-22. They either want to pay Uncle Sam as little as possible, or they are trying to do their general bookkeeping themselves when they should be using a CPA. Not accurately reporting your finances not only can keep you from getting loans from banks, it also can get you in trouble with the government and cost a lot more than you think you may be saving. Creating systems and getting the best quality advice in the area of finances will help you sleep better at night and give you more potential for profit than almost anything else.

4. TECHNOLOGY

It used to be that you could start a business with just a telephone and a fax machine. But today you need a computer, access to the Internet, a Web page (which must be protected from attack as well as updated regularly), and software to manage your accounting, client data, and work flow. Once you have made the initial investment in hardware and software, you also need to have systems to create, research, purchase, protect, update, and maintain your technology.

You need to manage the information you accumulate and make the best use of your customer data. So unless you have a little "computer nerd" inside you, or a son or daughter or nephew or neighborhood kid who's a whiz at technology, this is one area in which it pays to contract out from the start. Luckily, there are many moderately priced services that can help you. Start by talking with the salespeople when you buy your computers; there may be local technology services firms they recommend. Also talk with other business people and find out who they are using. As a last resort, you can check the local *Yellow Pages*. Just make sure you get, and check, references for any service professional you are thinking of using.

THE THIRD KEY FUNCTION: MARKETING AND SALES

The conventional wisdom used to be, "Build a better product or provide a better service, and the people will come." Well . . . not always. You have to *tell* them about your product or service before they will show up at your door. Your marketing and sales provide the consistent pipeline of business that will keep your doors open. The key word is *consistent*. You might get business without any marketing or sales systems, but your sales will definitely be inconsistent. And inconsistent sales do not make for long-term business.

There are three different components in your marketing and sales area: customer attraction, customer conversion, and customer retention.

1. CUSTOMER ATTRACTION

This includes identifying your ideal customers and then bringing your product or service to their attention. Included in customer attraction are your advertising and public relations. Your goal is to get the customers to come to you rather than your having to chase them.

2. CUSTOMER CONVERSION

Once you have attracted the customer's notice, you must convert interest into a sale. How easy do you make it for the customer to do business with you? How flexible are your payment options? Your delivery choices?

Are you equipped to satisfy both an impulse purchase and a considered sale?

3. Customer Retention

When you have made one sale, your customer retention functions move into action. Do you continue to treat customers as a valuable asset and source of referrals, or do they feel they've dropped off the face of the earth as soon as you have their money? What's your customer satisfaction policy? What about refunds? Do you have incentives for referrals or repeat business? The goal of all of your marketing and sales functions is to build a long-term relationship with each and every customer or client, creating excellent customer satisfaction, repeat business, and referrals.

THE FOURTH KEY FUNCTION: BUSINESS OPERATIONS

This is what most business owners know and do best, and so I usually spend very little time working with clients on this. I do suggest that business owners think ahead and plan for the future of their product or service. What will happen when your business starts to grow and other people are involved in delivering your product or service? How much information is only in your head and not on paper?

As you grow, you'll start delegating certain important tasks to other staff members. While you focus on your unique ability and your owner's responsibilities, you will start forgetting how to accomplish the tasks you have assigned to someone else. Now, imagine that key person leaves for whatever reason. Will you remember what needs to be done? You must start turning your unique way of doing things or producing products into written systems, including an *operations manual.*

Not too long ago I got a phone call from a worried client. She has a successful jewelry business, with two key employees who both had been with her at least five years. She trusted them implicitly, and she had delegated almost all of the functions of the business to them so that she could focus on designing and marketing her jewelry. In the same week, both employees—100 percent of her staff—gave notice. One employee's husband took a job in another state; the other employee's son had come down with a terrible illness, and she was going to have to stay home and take care of him.

The jewelry owner was waking up in the middle of the night in a cold sweat. My solution? I quickly got together two of my consultants to meet with her departing staff and document their job functions. Then we wrote an operations manual that included complete job descriptions and systems for running the business. We hired two new staff members and trained them with the written systems. The transition was easy and seamless.

Don't wait until a key person leaves your company. If your business systems are in your head and not written down, you are setting yourself up for a lot of pain. You need to create an operations manual at the same time you are building your business. That way, if you or any of your key employees get sick or have to be gone for any reason, others can take over their functions with relative ease.

Your operations manual should include information on three specific functions.

- *Research and development.* You should be working continually to upgrade and/or expand your products or services.

- *Production.* This includes the basics of creating your product or service.

- *Distribution.* This describes how your product or service reaches your end users or customers.

Once you have these functions described in your operations manual, your business can run successfully whether you're in the room or meeting with clients on the other side of the world. And it will give you a feeling of security and peace of mind like nothing else.

TURNING A BUSINESS BLUEPRINT
INTO A WORKING BUSINESS

Creating a business blueprint for your company can be a very liberating experience. It can turn the thousands and thousands of tasks that go into running a business into something that may not be easy but is at least manageable. When my clients create their own business blueprints, they usually say things like, "For the first time I feel like I'm in control. I know what to do to make the most of my time and energy. I feel like I'll be able to support my team and build my business a lot faster." Employees at companies where we have implemented business blueprints tell us they enjoy their work more than ever because their responsibilities are so clear.

Once you start to identify the number of daily activities that are required to run a business, you soon will understand that you need help. Of course, most new business owners have to be responsible for all of the functions of their businesses until they can create enough cash flow either to hire the right people or to outsource the work. That level of cash flow should be one of your first goals. Only when you are doing enough business to hire others to take care of some of your business functions (ideally the ones you don't enjoy or aren't very good at) can you start to build a business that will be part of your life instead of all of your life. That's why your business blueprint also identifies who will be ultimately responsible for those major functions.

When I first started both of my small businesses, I did everything by myself. Now my current business, Louis Barajas Wealth & Business Planning, employs nine people and will be expanding again in the near future. But when I look at the business blueprint I use today, the areas of focus are exactly the same as when I was both the business owner and sole employee. In chapter 10, we'll talk about using these areas of focus to help you build a team that will give you greater results with far less effort on your part.

Your business blueprint also can be a valuable tool in keeping track of who performs the different functions and systems in the different areas.

The business blueprint for Louis Barajas Wealth & Business Planning is color-coded to show who is responsible for what. When we first opened our doors, most of the blueprint was blue, which meant I was responsible for most of the tasks. Later, Aaron, another financial planner, took over more functions; then Gilbert came on as an intern (he's now a junior partner); then Angie, my wife, and Eddie, my stepson, started working in the business. Eventually we added other advisors, outside consultants, and so on. Now the only blue on the chart is up at the top, in the "owner" area and in the consulting area of our firm. And I'm looking at ways I can share some of those functions with key members of my team.

WORKING ON YOUR BUSINESS
TO CREATE SYSTEMS AND A TEAM

The next two chapters might seem somewhat daunting, especially for first-time entrepreneurs. Take heart! My goal is to simplify things for you, not complicate them. While I'll be using "business" language, I will also give you several examples so you can relate the information to your own small business. In chapter 7 we said that thinking is some of the toughest work we can do, and that's why so few people do it. For the next few pages you're going to need to think a little and apply what you read to your own circumstances. Instead of working *in* your business, you're going to work *on* your business. But just like an architect's blueprint makes it possible for a builder to erect your house in the most efficient manner, learning to draw a blueprint for your business will allow you to build it in the most efficient and effective manner as well.

In chapter 9, we'll talk about the specific systems in each area, and I will give you some suggestions for implementing these systems, whether you are a one-person shop or a good-sized small business. But my hope is that, by understanding how to build an efficient and effective business right from the start, your chances of success will be far greater and you will be able to weather the challenges that every small business inevitably faces. By creating a businesslike structure to support your vision, you're giving yourself a much better chance of building a small business and a big life.

9

STEP 4: Your Business Systems

Make It Easy to Build Success

A system is a way of making functions automatic. To create a system, you look at things you need to do and come up with ways of doing them that take less effort and focus because you don't have to think about them all the time. A system allows you to simplify your workload and become more efficient. Creating systems for your business blueprint functions will allow you to walk into your business on the first day, roll up your sleeves, and say, "Let's go to work." You will have the confidence to put your business together in such a way that it will run fairly smoothly from the start.

Let me give you an example of a simple system. An attorney told me he was frustrated because clients were telling him he never returned their phone calls. He was tired of playing phone tag with people and having his work time constantly interrupted by his secretary asking him to take calls. We set up a system where he would return all phone calls between 1:30 and 2:30 P.M. If someone called at other times, his secretary would say, "Mr. Muñoz will call you between 1:30 and 2:30 P.M. tomorrow. Can you give me a number where you can be reached at that time?" The attorney was happy because he could get his work done, and his clients felt that their calls were being returned in a timely manner.

I travel frequently, and I use a system to help me pack. It used to be that I'd get to my destination and discover I'd forgotten toothpaste or hair gel or some other toiletry item. It wasn't the end of the world, but replacing it was an unnecessary hassle. Now I keep a checklist in my travel bag. When I'm packing for a trip I consult the list, pack all the items on it, and I'm ready to go. I don't have to think about packing because I have created a system to help me.

If you have to do everything yourself, you do not own a business—you own a job. If you're ever going to remove yourself from the drudgery of having to do everything yourself, you will need to create and implement systems. Systems make key functions duplicable. That means instead of your having to do everything yourself, other people can do the same tasks and create the same results, like following a recipe. Most real estate companies have a system for estimating the value of a house. Their system has been automated to a point where a Realtor can walk in your door, open his or her laptop, and walk around checking off the various elements of your home that increase or decrease its value. Extra bathroom? Check. Redone kitchen? Check. Small backyard? Check. Needs new carpet? Check. Then they can go online to see what other homes in the neighborhood are selling for, hit a button, and give you a very accurate assessment of what your home is worth in the current market. Anyone who becomes a Realtor can be trained to use this system. It makes one key element of the realty business completely duplicable. You, too, can create replicable systems in your business so you can have both a business and a life outside of it.

Working on your business systems is about creating a specific mind-set. It's focusing on strategic work, not just tactical work. Creating systems can eventually free you from the shackles of "having to do it all"—one of the most common complaints of most small business owners. Systems also allow you to focus on what you love to do and what you're great at doing. As a result, you're more likely to keep the passion with which you started the business. In addition, developing systems allows you to identify the unique abilities of your employees so that you can give them the opportunity to handle the areas of business that you don't want to—or should not have to—manage.

SYSTEMS ARE THE KEY TO GROWTH

Most of our clients just want to create a business that minimizes their frustrations and creates profits, allowing them to enjoy going into work each day while they balance their lives with things they love most, like spending time with their families. But you need to plan for growth in your business if you want it to be around for the long term.

Systems are your key to orderly, manageable growth. I have heard from countless individuals that if you are not growing in life, you are dying. This also relates to your business. I don't want you to think that you must expand your company until it's the size of a Wal-Mart or Microsoft, or even open more than one facility or branch. But if you did, your systems will help you do that and stay sane. Creating the right systems also will allow you to focus on planning for business growth instead of being caught up in your daily workload.

In the last chapter we talked about the four key functions for every company: the owner's responsibilities, internal operations, marketing and sales, and business operations. In this chapter, you will learn about the different systems that enable those functions to run smoothly. I'm not going to go into a lot of detail; some very talented specialists have entire books about each of the four key areas. (I like Conrad Levinson and Philip Kotler on marketing, Peter Drucker's management books, and Eric Tyson's *Small Business for Dummies* for business structure and systems.) However, in this chapter I will discuss the systems that are required for every small business.

I also want to show you that creating systems is not complicated. I'll give examples of elegant systems that can be created in just a few minutes to handle some of your most important business frustrations.

In the same way that creating a small business, big life requires that you put in the time to create both a life blueprint and business blueprint, you also will need to make time to work on your systems. Especially at first, this can feel like a waste of time. How can you take an hour away from contacting customers, selling your product or service, and getting everything else accomplished that's screaming to be done (along with doing all the other things that are part of living, like spending time with your family, taking care of your health, commuting, sleeping, eating)? But in the same way that you must spend time planning and drawing the blueprint for your business before you open your doors, you must continue working on your systems in order to keep growing.

You might have read Albert Einstein's quote: "The definition of insanity is doing the same thing over and over and expecting different results." As I told the young woman with the custom closet business, if you're too busy to work on your business rather than in it, then you're just too busy. Time is all about priorities (as Stephen Covey says, making the important urgent). If you feel you don't have the time to work on your systems, it's probably because you're focusing on the day-to-day running of your business. And if you keep doing that, you'll never have the time to get better.

Other than, creating a life blueprint, devising and implementing business systems is the most powerful thing that you can do to create a small business, big life.

You will find this chapter is easier to follow if you make a copy of the business blueprint on page 109 and use it as your guide as we discuss the different areas of focus. Or you can go to my Web site, www.louisbarajas.com, enter the "Small Business, Big Life" area, and print out a larger copy of the business blueprint as a reference. Make sure you are reading this section with a pad of paper and pencil to write down any ideas for systems that will work in your own business.

(If you want more information or coaching, you can attend one of our workshops on developing your small business systems. In our workshops, we share with each other innovative ideas to help broaden our views of how small business can operate to give us more success and more life. See our Web site for seminar details and dates.)

Let's start with the owner's systems. These are the systems that will make your job as the owner easier, more enjoyable, *and* more productive!

THE OWNER'S SYSTEMS

As the owner, working on your business means developing, evaluating, and refining the systems that allow your business to operate and prosper. You should block off a certain amount of time to think and plan. This can be an hour a week, a half-hour a day, an hour over the weekend—whatever works best for your schedule. But you must treat your appointment for "thinking time" as seriously as you treat an appointment with your most important client.

Turn off your phone, stay away from your e-mail, and hang a "Do Not Disturb" sign on your door. I actually stay at home for my own planning sessions because I get interrupted so much at the office. This can sometimes be uncomfortable. Your employees may not understand why you are unavailable. But this is some of the most important time you can spend when it comes to the long-term success of your business.

As part of thinking about your business, you also should spend time learning about ways to do what you do even better. Make a point to read books, go to seminars, and take classes. The Small Business Administration (SBA) and the Small Business Development Corporation (SBDC) offer free or low-cost courses on how to start a business. Courses and books will not only increase your knowledge about your business but also will give you different and fresh perspectives on what you're doing. There's a wonderful scene in the movie *Dead Poet's Society*. Robin Williams is an unorthodox teacher at a boys' prep school. One day, he has each of the boys come to the front of the room and stand on top of his desk. "You have a very different perspective from up there," he says. You, too, should try to discover new ways of doing things and new ways of looking at what you are already doing. This will help keep your business (and you) learning and growing.

Here is a short description of some of the systems you can put in place to assist you in fulfilling the three responsibilities of an owner: compliance, "big picture" thinking (vision, culture development, company growth), and systems development.

A. COMPLIANCE

Legal compliance for any business is mandatory. I suggest that you find a business attorney who focuses on your specific industry and meet with him or her to review your legal risks. (A good business attorney will be part of your "outside" team, as we will discuss in chapter 10.) You also should schedule an annual meeting with your attorney to discuss legal issues that can or will affect your business. I set this annual meeting as a recurring event on my computer calendar.

Insurance compliance is another necessary component. You need to work with an insurance agent that specializes in businesses. Depending on your industry and situation, some insurance policies might be mandatory while others are highly recommended. You should review your insurance needs regularly in order to cover workers' compensation, liability, errors and omissions, auto, health, life, disability, and more. Schedule a meeting with your insurance agent to discuss your needs and review your premiums. Make this meeting an annual recurring event on your calendar.

B. "BIG PICTURE" THINKING

- *Vision.* A system for visioning is the process of *visualization.* Make time to reflect, or dream, or think about what your company would look like if it were completed and perfect. I schedule one day every quarter out of the office in an inspiring location to dream about my life and my company.

- *Culture Development.* "Culture" is a sociological term meaning how people behave. Every group has a culture; in most small businesses the culture is a reflection of the owner first and employees second. As the owner, you will set the tone for your company right from the beginning, and culture development must be an ongoing focus as well. What systems could you put in place to create a positive culture for your company? How will you foster that positive culture year after year?

One of my clients schedules a quarterly team building event for his staff. This client bought a book on team building and uses the exercises from the book. Other means of culture development include a business mission statement, code of conduct, regular employee meetings to handle issues, an "open-door" policy (one afternoon a month when you as the owner are available to anyone for a chat), and so on.

- *Company Growth.* There are three different categories of systems that will help you monitor and plan for company growth. First, you need a system to monitor *customer capacity.* How many clients or customers can you handle given your current resources? There's nothing worse than failing to satisfy a customer's needs simply because you do not have the product in stock or enough time or people to get the job done as promised.

   Second, you need to monitor your *accounts receivable aging schedule* and *cash flow projections* to see how cash flow is being handled. This will help you avoid the kind of cash crunch that has sunk many an otherwise prosperous business.

   Finally, you want to create a system to do periodic *cost analysis of your pricing or fees.* If the materials that go into your product are getting more expensive or if the industry standard for the services you offer is higher or lower than your current rates, you need to be able to adjust your pricing accordingly. A good accountant or business consultant can help you set up these systems, and then you must put into your calendar periodic and regular reviews of the results.

C. SYSTEMS DEVELOPMENT AND REVIEW

You need to reserve time each week to focus on making your company better. This includes time to review your current systems to see if you can improve upon them, or develop new ones that will allow you to grow. Doing this will give you a competitive edge. I have developed a simple way to make this kind of thinking easier. I ask my clients to track their creative energy throughout the day or week. Some of my clients are more creative in the morning, others in the afternoon. Some are more creative on specific days of the workweek. We track that for a week and find their creative zone and then block off a couple of hours a week during that time for them to work on systems development.

INTERNAL OPERATIONS SYSTEMS

As you recall, internal operations include human resources, general administration, finance, and technology. This part of a company tends to be systematized early in a business's evolution. However, it is very easy for a start-up business to miss putting a system in place, only to pay the price for it later. I suggest you use the following list as a guide for systematizing your internal operations. If you have systems in these areas already, congratulations! If not, take the time to create them—preferably before you actually need them.

A. Human Resources

There are six systems you should consider creating for the people in your company. Whether you have one employee or many, you will need to have these systems in place to support current and future growth.

- *Recruiting.* Where will you find future employees? How will you screen them? Should you use an outside recruiter or headhunter or do it yourself? Create a single written page of the places and contacts to use when you need to hire employees.

- *Hiring.* Do you already know what you will be looking for in your employees? Do you have interview questions written in advance? Who else needs to be involved in making the hiring decisions? How much latitude do you have to negotiate salary and benefits? What kind of benefits package do you provide? How long do you anticipate it will be between offering someone a job and actually putting him or her to work?

Creating a written system for hiring will not only make your life easier now (assuming you will be doing all the hiring when you first start your business), but it will also make things smoother and clearer later when other people in your company or an outside human resource consultant will be part of the hiring process.

- *Employee training.* Once you make the decision to hire an employee, do you have a written document outlining training procedures? Will you provide specific and/or continuing education for your employees? Do you have a training manual? To help you create a business that will be around for the long term, I suggest that every employee have a written job description and a list of the duties required in the job.

Do you remember the jewelry store owner described in chapter 8, who lost her only two employees at the same time? We spent a week documenting everything her employees did so that we could create job descriptions and systems for their positions. Don't wait until someone leaves you in the lurch; set up your training systems now, and you will save yourself a lot of grief later.

- *Compliance.* When you hire an employee, he or she will need to fill out an I-9 Form, a W-4 Form, an employment agreement, health insurance form, and more. Do you have a list of all the forms you will need an employee to complete? Do you have an employee handbook? A handbook will cover legal issues, insurance requirements, time clock and work hour regulations, other labor regulations that apply to your business, safety procedures, how to deal with harassment and other complaint procedures, and more.

We recently saw a client with ten employees, and she had violated time clock and overtime procedures. Her business was fined over $45,000 by the U.S. Department of Labor. I highly recommend hiring a human resource consultant for advice in this area. The benefits will definitely outweigh the costs.

- *Evaluation.* What formal written evaluation systems do you have? How often are employees given performance reviews? Do you have clear written descriptions of what employees can expect from evaluations and how often these meetings will occur? How do you determine raises and bonuses, and what do you communicate to your employees? You can purchase prewritten evaluation systems from human resource product companies, but you must put the systems in place in your company.

- *Termination.* What's your system for warning employees about issues that arise with their work? Do you keep documented records of complaints? What actions are grounds for immediate termination, and what actions will result in a warning? What's your process for meeting with employees and informing them of any challenges? (In today's litigious society, you'd better get everything in writing and have the employee sign it, to save yourself from an unlawful termination lawsuit.) Do you know what the employee's rights are if you terminate him or her? What's your procedure for employees who are departing, whether it's their choice or yours? Do you have a checklist of the items you will need an employee to return if he or she is terminated?

  When I started my first business, I had an employee who had done something unethical, so I fired her. When she left, I forgot that she had a key to our front door. A checklist would have reminded me to get back the key. Instead, I had to hire a locksmith to change all the locks.

As I said in chapter 8, while these tasks may seem daunting, there are companies and consultants who can handle many of your HR functions. Making sure all of your human resource functions are handled, and handled well, will make the difference between a company that people want to work for and one they avoid because it seems slipshod and risky. When you take care of the needs of your employees, you will strengthen your company's foundation.

B. GENERAL ADMINISTRATION

These are the functions that help the business of your business to flow smoothly. They're the little things that may not seem to make a difference—until there are problems!

- *Reception.* It is often said that the receptionist is the "Director of First Impressions" for your company. You need to have systems to monitor how he or she answers the phone, the amount of time clients spend on hold, and so on. You may be surprised to learn that sometimes the first source of frustration your customers or clients have with your company is how the phone is being answered. What are your systems for monitoring this important detail? For example, at our company I don't like anyone to be put on hold for more than ten seconds. We have a small clock with a timer sitting directly in front of our receptionist, so whoever answers the phone always will know how long a client is on hold.

  Another system I use to see how my receptionist answers the phone is to call our general phone number when I am out of the office instead of the direct line to one of my staff, so I can hear how the receptionist is performing. I also insist that all our staff state the company name and their own names when answering the phone.

- *Secretarial Services.* Your general administrative person usually has many tasks—purchasing office supplies, mailing letters and bills, writing letters, helping answer phones, and sometimes making deliveries or picking up items for the business. Because this area is often neglected, there are usually huge inefficiencies due to lack of attention and poor training.

Pay attention to how your general administrative roles are handled. Make sure the people who do these tasks are focused on what's important, not just on what is urgent. A simple but extremely effective system is to have your general administrative person write down and prioritize his or her most important tasks for the day. This employee also should help with cost containment—comparing costs for office products, delivery services, and so on. A great administrative person can save you a lot of time and money if he or she is properly trained and taught how to think systematically.

C. Finance

Here are the five different kinds of systems you must put into place to keep track of the financial side of your business.

- *Accounting.* What accounting software is best for the needs for your company? There are software packages that are easy to use, like QuickBooks, and some that are made specifically for different industries. You will need to know in advance if your business will have accrual or cash accounting. My suggestion is to consult an accountant who specializes in your industry and knows which software would be best for you.

  You also need to set up a system to review your financial statements (income statement, balance sheet, cash flow statement) periodically. I used to be in business with a CPA and noticed that most of our clients rarely reviewed their financial statements—they just didn't understand them or have the time to review them. That's a big mistake. Financial statements are essential to the financial health of your business.

  I have created a tool to help with interpreting financial statements. We call it the Financial Health Dashboard™. The gauges on the dashboard of a car are designed to tell you at a glance about the most important measures of your car's performance. In a second you can tell how fast the car is going, how high the engine is revving (RPMs), how hot it's running, and how much gas you have. If you need gas or the engine's running hot, you can take care of the problem before things get serious. In the same way, most business owners only need to focus on four or five measures of company performance to know how things are going. The Financial Health Dashboard worksheet allows us to capture the four or five most important numbers from the financial statements, so the owner can tell at a glance how well his company is performing. (To learn more about the Financial Health Dashboard, please go to www.louisbarajas.com.)

- *Regulatory filings.* Ask your accountant to review with you the regulatory financial filing requirements for your business. Some forms may need to be filed monthly, quarterly, and/or annually. On your calendar, mark the deadlines for each form as a recurring event.

- *Billing and collection.* I've worked with countless clients who lose thousands of dollars a year because of the lack of billing systems. If you sell "cash and carry," obviously you won't have this problem. But if you bill for your work or service, you need to establish efficient and effective systems. Ask other people in your industry how they handle their billing. Once again, a good accountant who knows your industry is a great resource.

- *Payroll.* This is one of the most neglected and problematic areas for a business owner because the laws change rapidly and it's hard to keep up with current rules. There are many great resources for handling this function. I recommend that most small businesses hire a company like ADP or Paychex to take over payroll. Payroll companies do all payroll reporting and file all paperwork with regulatory agencies (both IRS and state). They also will pay any fines and/or penalties if their reporting is inaccurate.

- *Taxes.* Systemizing your tax payments, whether they're business taxes, employee taxes, or personal taxes, will make your life easier and your business run more smoothly. Just like regulatory filing, taxes are an area where you should hire professional assistance, if at all possible, because even a small mistake can come back to haunt you for many years. I suggest that every business owner hire a tax specialist to prepare their business tax returns.

D. TECHNOLOGY

You need to have systems to create, research, purchase, update, and maintain the three systems described below. As I said in chapter 8, unless technology is one of your strengths, you should hire someone to handle this area for you or find an outside service.

- *Hardware.* This includes any kind of machine required to operate your business, such as telephones, cell phones, computers, printers, copiers, cash registers, fax, postage meter, employee time clock, etc.

- *Software.* This includes computer networking software, financial software, business software, and customer database management software. Simply keeping up with software updates, upgrades, and security patches can be a full-time job. Most of your software will undoubtedly be "off the shelf" at first. As your business grows, however, you may need customized programs, or you may find yourself creating proprietary software as part of your products or services.

- *Information systems.* Most small business owners today are aware of the fact that customer information is one of the most valuable assets they possess. Therefore, using and protecting this information is critical. All it takes is one computer crash or hacker attack to ruin your business. Regular maintenance and protection of your information systems are absolutely essential. This category includes client data management, financial reporting information, and employee files.

MARKETING AND SALES SYSTEMS

There are many different ways to describe how your business will interact with your clients or customers. I prefer a simple, three-stage approach: (1) attracting the customer, (2) converting interest into a sale or contract, and (3) retaining the customer over the long term. You will need to create, update, and maintain systems for all three stages.

A. CUSTOMER ATTRACTION

Nine out of ten small businesses lack consistent marketing and sales systems. They have no referral program and no consistent way of reaching customers; they don't even know who their ideal customer is. They're like my young friend from Florida with the custom closet business. When I asked what her marketing plan was, she didn't have one. Then I asked her a follow-up question: "Who are your ideal clients? They can't be people your own age because custom closets are expensive and most twenty-three-year-olds can't afford it." She replied that her usual clients were in their late thirties to early forties, but she had never done any research on the best ways to reach them.

One of the first suggestions I make to my clients is that they identify the ideal customer profile for their product or service. I recommended to the custom closet business owner that she get together a group of friends and acquaintances who were the same age as her ideal client and turn them into a mini-focus group. "Ask them who they are, what they like to do, where they shop, with whom they socialize, what they buy, and what other services they utilize," I said. "Find out which magazines they read, which television shows they watch, and which Web sites they visit regularly. Get as much information as you can that will help you put your company in front of the right people in the right way." Once a business owner knows this kind of information about the company's ideal customer, it's much easier to put any marketing efforts where they will do the greatest good.

You also need to ask, "Why should someone do business with me?" And don't say, "Because of our superior service, product, or price." Everyone says that. Take the time to truly answer that question in order to differentiate your product or service from the competition.

Some marketing books recommend that you come up with a "thirty second elevator speech," putting your unique selling points into one or two sentences. Whatever answer you come up with, do your best to be clear as to why people should want to do business with you rather than the business owner down the street.

When I ask business owners about their best source of attracting customers, 80 percent will say "referrals from other customers." Yet when I ask them to tell me about their system for creating a consistent flow of referrals, they just say, "There's no system really—our clients just refer us to their friends." You can survive in business "hoping" someone is going to refer new customers to you, or you can create a referral system that, when executed consistently, creates a consistent flow of business.

Some people spend thousands of dollars on ineffective advertising when a referral system would produce many more potential clients. Publicity and referrals (third-party endorsements) are the most cost effective methods of attracting customers.

B. CUSTOMER CONVERSION

Have you ever found a product you liked and wanted, but the business made it difficult for you to buy? They don't have it in stock, for example, or they don't take credit cards, or they don't take cash. It is one of the most frustrating things a customer can experience. If you want to turn a potential customer into a purchasing customer, especially given the rise of the Internet and global business outreach, you need to establish systems that enable you to do business easily and efficiently with anyone in the world.

Let's say that you have attracted a customer. How easy do you make it for that potential client to buy from you the first day? Do you have a contract or product ready to go? What's your conversion process? Is it consistent? Do you have systems to accept payment by credit cards? Can clients make purchases through your Web site? Do you have inventory systems to check when you are running low on a certain product? Persuading clients to buy is hard enough; you need to make it as easy as possible for them to do business when they are ready to do so.

C. CUSTOMER RETENTION

There's a story about a man who dies and goes to purgatory. In purgatory he meets the devil, who asks him if he wants to go to hell. At the same time, St. Peter arrives to invite the man to heaven. The devil tells the man, "Hey, don't make up your mind until you take a quick tour of hell—you might be pleasantly surprised at what you see."

The man goes to hell and gets a personal tour from the devil. He sees men and women playing volleyball on a beach, sipping margaritas and having a good time. He goes back up to purgatory and requests a tour of heaven from St. Peter. In heaven he sees people in white robes, playing harps and looking kind of bored. The man tells the devil and St. Peter that he needs to sleep on his decision.

The next day the man decides to go to hell. But once he arrives in hell, it's completely changed. The good-looking men and women are gone, and instead of a beach there's nothing but fire and brimstone. He sees the devil and asks, "What happened? Where are the people having a good time? Where are the margaritas? Where's the party?"

The devil says, "Yesterday you were a prospect. Today you're a client."

How often do small business owners treat new customers that way? We promise them the world if they will buy our product or service, but once they've bought we forget about them or don't follow through with our promises. Nearly every major marketing study comes to the same conclusion: it is much cheaper to keep clients than to lose them and have to replace them. The same studies reveal that most unsatisfied clients will tell seven to ten people about their unhappiness with your company. You need to create systems that will provide consistent and exceptional customer service.

As a business owner, you should gather focus groups of people like your ideal customers and walk them through your process of client attraction, conversion, and referral. Ask them to be honest with you about what they like and what they dislike, what they find effective or ineffective. Seeing things from an outside perspective is probably the most valuable perspective you can get.

BUSINESS OPERATIONS SYSTEMS

The following three areas are what you undoubtedly know best about your business. I won't go any into any detail with these, but I will remind you that you need to document your business systems even if you can recite them from memory. Remember, the only way you will ever be able to have both a small business and a life, much less a big one, is if your operation can run without your being there.

A. Research and Development

No matter what your product or service, you must always be working to upgrade your current offerings and bring new ideas and material into the business. This area is often tied closely to your vision for the future, and if R&D is not part of your vision, make it so.

B. Production

This is how you create the product or deliver the service the client is paying for. Having written systems and guidelines for production will (1) make your business duplicable, (2) allow you to expand when you're ready, and (3) let you sleep more easily at night, knowing that if you get hit on the head and wind up with amnesia, you will still have a business to come back to.

C. Distribution

Your product or service does no one any good if it is sitting on the shelves in your warehouse or stuck in the mail somewhere. How do you get your products to your customers, whether they are end users or other businesses that sell and/or distribute your wares? Having clear systems, as well as back-ups for your distribution systems, will help you overcome challenges that are outside your control, like bad weather, natural disasters, and computer crashes.

AUTOMATING YOUR SYSTEMS

In *The Automatic Millionaire*, David Bach states that, to achieve financial independence, people need to automate their personal financial planning strategies. I believe that if you are going to achieve a successful small business, big life, you must do the same thing for your business systems.

Automating your systems will create consistent experiences for your customers. It will also build certainty in your employees, giving them a firm ground upon which to build a strong team. Once your systems are automatic, you as the owner will have the confidence that your business can run with or without you in the office all the time. You can do more of what you love and more of what you have a gift for. And you probably will enjoy your business much more as a result.

One way to automate your systems is to leverage, or delegate, them to others. At the beginning, of course, most entrepreneurs do almost everything themselves. (They usually have to!) But eventually, you will start to build a team of inside and outside associates who can take over some of the functions. In the next chapter, we will talk about building a strong team of great employees and contractors who share your vision and who love what they do for your company.

How do you know your systems are working? You need to create key numbers, a measurement, to evaluate your systems for success. You can quantify just about anything, including qualitative measures like "happy clients." Remember that the key functions of your business will work only if you build practical, automated systems to create consistent experiences for yourself, your suppliers, your employees, and most importantly, your customers.

10

STEP 5: Your Team

The Bigger the Dream,
the Better the Team Needed

No one can be good at everything. Remember in chapter 4 we spoke of identifying your own strengths and weaknesses when it comes to your business? You can try to strengthen your weaknesses, but usually all you get are strong weaknesses. If you're not strong in finances, for example, you can study accounting, but you probably won't enjoy it and you won't be good at it either. You won't be using your *don,* your unique gift, and you probably won't be either fulfilled or successful.

As a business owner, you need to start with your own unique gift, then take a look at your business blueprint and say, "Which functions am I great at? Which functions do I love? Which functions or areas am I really bad at? What do I absolutely hate to do?" And instead of trying to be something you're not, you should manage your weaknesses and play to your strengths by building a strong team of inside and outside players (employees and contractors). You do what you are great at and let your team do the things at which they excel.

One of the biggest problems that I see are with small business owners who think that they can do it alone, or they tell me that they can't find the right help. But as the title of this chapter says, the bigger the dream, the better the team needed. Some consultants will tell you, "Small business is like a McDonald's. As long as you have great systems, you can hire pretty much anybody." But I don't agree. You can have incredible systems, but you also need the right people. Your associates, both inside and outside your company, will make or break you. Therefore, you must learn to build the best team possible.

However, you can't build a great team until you know the skills and abilities your business requires. That's why building a great team is the last stage in building a small business, big life. Once your life blueprint is in place, once you have created a business blueprint that describes all the functions of your business, and once you have devised the systems to make those functions run smoothly, you're now ready to hire the people who will bring that plan to life.

Everyone has different gifts, and creating a business blueprint and the corresponding systems will allow you to apportion the functions of your business to those who will do a great job with them. A business blueprint allows your entire staff to see the functions required in order for the business to run well. It clarifies the roles each person is expected to play, what they have to do within that role, what they are responsible for, whom to ask if questions arise, and how the entire team can interact to build an exceptional business.

Instead of putting the wrong people in the wrong place and making your job more difficult, you can lead a team of people who are able to express their unique gifts in their work, which will give them more fulfillment and will give you a much higher performing team.

WHAT'S YOUR TEAM'S K.A.S.H.?

How do you identify the gifts of your current and future employees? Dan Sullivan, author of *The Laws of Lifetime Growth*, came up with the acronym K.A.S.H. to indicate what you should look for. It stands for *knowledge, abilities, skills,* and *habits. Knowledge* is the information required by the position. A bookkeeper, for instance, must have specialized knowledge in basic accounting. Now, almost anyone could be trained in that knowledge, but ideally your bookkeeper also would have *ability* with figures. Some people are good with numbers, while other people get frustrated trying to balance a checkbook. If you put the latter person in a bookkeeping job, it would not be a good fit.

You also want your bookkeeper to have *skills* that will help him or her to do the job. Skills might include using the computer program you have chosen for your bookkeeping. If necessary, you can train people in the skills of a position, but it will take longer for them to get up to speed. Finally, your bookkeeper should have work *habits* that help him or her do the job well.

Good bookkeepers are organized, neat, punctual, detail oriented; they will not rest until the books are balanced and the financial statements are accurate. A good bookkeeper does not need to be gregarious or outgoing. But what if you tried to put your bookkeeper into a sales job? You would probably have immaculate records of how many sales were made and how much money came in, but your actual sales would probably go down unless the bookkeeper had the K.A.S.H. required of a great salesperson. If someone is in the right job, they're using their K.A.S.H. to the fullest.

You can train people in knowledge and skills, but it's somewhat harder to train habits, and difficult indeed to change abilities. Ability is tied to your unique gift. Your goal as a business owner is to put employees into jobs where their abilities are used to their fullest, where they have the knowledge and skill to do a great job, as well as the habits that will help them succeed.

When someone joins our company, we ask them to take the assessment test from the book *Now, Discover Your Strengths* by Marcus Buckingham and Donald Clifton, to help determine their K.A.S.H. This helps us discover if (1) they're suited for the position based on abilities, (2) they need training in knowledge or skills to help them do a great job, and (3) there are any potential problems with habits that must be monitored.

To put together a world-class team, you need to hire people based on their K.A.S.H., not based on affection, family ties, or favors. This can be difficult, especially at first. Most business owners hire friends and family members as their first employees because they are accessible, they are known commodities, and they usually accept the vision of the business because of their relationship with the owner. However, hiring friends and family sometimes results in people doing jobs for which they are minimally capable and often unsuited. Worse yet, people bring with them the feelings from their personal relationships with the owner outside.

If you need to utilize family members and/or friends as employees, I suggest you have them do some kind of K.A.S.H. assessment. If nothing else, this may give them a better idea of what their strengths and weaknesses are in terms of employment, which can be helpful whether they work for you or another company. It also will give you some helpful information as to how best to use the talents of this friend/family member. Whether you are employing a spouse, child, parent, cousin, friend, or former teacher, he or she will do a better job, and both of you will be happier, if the jobs suit his or her skills and abilities.

Talents don't become strengths until they are put to use in the right environment. If you already own a business, I suggest you give your current employees a K.A.S.H. assessment test and then ask yourself, "Is this person in the right job? Are some of the things I'm asking him or her to do unsuited to his or her strengths?"

When we did assessments of everyone in our office, we were surprised to find that some people were mismatched for their functions. So we reshuffled responsibilities to give people the tasks that suited their K.A.S.H. Today our employees are flourishing. They enjoy what they do, and they're producing great results. As our company grows and we add people to our team, we always evaluate their K.A.S.H. as part of the hiring process. Giving people work to do that allows them to express their *don*, their unique gift—which is represented by their knowledge, abilities, skills, and habits—means greater fulfillment for them and greater success for your business.

WHEN AND HOW TO DELEGATE

Once you know your team's K.A.S.H., you can use this information to fill in the boxes on your business blueprint. Take a look at your employees and ask, "What are their unique abilities? What do they love to do, and what are they great at doing? Based on that, what functions can they handle, and where would they not do well?"

When you're first starting out, you may have very few people handling a lot of functions, and it won't be possible for your employees (or you) to do only the things that suit their unique abilities. Whenever possible, however, you should match the function with people who have that ability, even if it does not fall under their usual job description or if they do not yet have all the training they need to fill the job. I would rather have my stepson, Eddie, working on PowerPoint slides for one of my presentations than try to do them myself, because Eddie loves working with computers and he's good at it. Spending money to train Eddie to use PowerPoint is a great investment. Spending the same amount of money to train me would be less effective.

When we developed the business blueprint for Louis Barajas Wealth & Business Planning, the color-coded chart indicated who was responsible for what. In the beginning, there were three colors, representing Aaron, Gilbert, and me. As we expanded the business and added more employees, we added colors. As the new employees were able to take on more functions, the amount of blue (my color) on the chart decreased.

As we grew, I could delegate a lot more of the business functions and focus on the areas that I as the owner needed to cover. If anyone came to me with a technology issue, for example, I could say, "Take a look at our business blueprint—I'm not the one who owns that area. Go talk to this person—he's in charge of technology." Delegating functions in this way was a huge relief to me. Problems were solved faster, and jobs were done by the people best suited to do them.

Delegating means sharing not just responsibility but also information and, to a certain degree, ownership. Some business owners resist sharing this kind of knowledge because they're afraid to give out too much information.

I had a client whose phone card and money wire transfer business had been struggling for a while, but things finally had started to get better. He came to me for advice on how to handle a planned expansion to another store. "I can see two potential problems," I told him. "You don't have an employee handbook, and you're missing some critical documents for your employees. I'd suggest you bring in an HR consultant and look for someone in-house that you can train to handle those functions."

The client looked uncomfortable. "You know, I have two wonderful people who are helping me run the business, but if I train them to handle the HR stuff, they may learn something that would cost me."

"Like what?" I asked.

"Well, sometimes they work five to ten minutes of overtime. If they knew I was supposed to pay them time-and-a-half for that, they might use it against me."

To my mind, this owner was cutting off his nose to spite his face. For the sake of a few dollars an hour, he was keeping two wonderful employees from doing the best job they could. Because of his fear, the owner wasn't able to delegate a lot of jobs he could have gotten off his own plate. And underneath it all, he was fostering an atmosphere of distrust and lack of confidence. I bet that his employees will eventually leave to work somewhere else—not because they could make more money but because they will feel more like a part of a team at another workplace.

If you are ever going to grow, you will need the support of a strong, dedicated team who believes in your business, your mission, and you, as well as in their own abilities to get the job done. Oftentimes, people will do more for a team and for others than they will ever do for themselves. When you create the feeling of a team in your workplace, you will tap into more power, commitment, expertise, and just plain heart than you can get in any other way.

Creating a strong team and letting others handle parts of your business blueprint does not mean abdicating your responsibility for the functions. As the owner, the buck stops with you. You need to be able to delegate authority while retaining the responsibility for running the business. Checking in with your employees on a regular basis is critical.

By using the business blueprint, you can check on whether functions are being handled instead of what specific tasks your employees are accomplishing. You will be managing from a healthier perspective, one that will allow you to keep your business running while ensuring your team is operating at top efficiency and effectiveness.

YOUR BUSINESS SUPPORT TEAM

When it comes to your business, you are only as strong as your weakest link. When I walk into a business that's been around for a while but is still struggling, the first questions I ask are, "Who's your accountant? Who's your banker? What consultants are you using? Who are your strategic partners?" All too often, they'll tell me that their accountant is really a bookkeeper who works part-time and the rest of the week he's a travel agent. They don't have an attorney because they've never been sued (luckily), and they've never even met the manager of their bank.

In the same way that you need a strong team inside your business, you need to build an equally strong team of outside supporters to give your business a solid foundation within your own community. To grow a business, you must enlist professionals who know how to help you. You must build your *business support team*.

The idea of a business support team can be difficult to embrace, especially when you first start a business, for two reasons. First, you may not know you need their services. You may not think you need an attorney or marketer or a janitorial service, until something comes up and you're in a bind. Then you will feel like a homeowner whose kitchen sink clogs up on the weekend during a dinner party and you are stuck paying a premium to get someone, anyone, to come to your house and fix it. That's not a situation you want to be in with your business! I hope that by reading the previous chapters you have increased your knowledge of what it takes to run a business successfully.

The second reason comes down to cost. Money is almost always tight when you are just starting out, so you could be tempted to say something like, "I can't afford an accountant, so I'm going to buy QuickBooks, read ten accounting books, and learn how to be an accountant." But if you're going to do that, why not just open up an accounting business?

There are only so many hours in a day, a week, and a year; it would be far better to build a small business that expresses your God-given talents than to waste your time and energy trying to save a very small amount of money. Instead, decide right up front to invest in the expertise of others. Take advantage of their unique abilities so that you can take advantage of your own.

The first and most important member of your "outside" team is not a businessperson—it's your spouse or significant other. I put "outside" in quotation marks because (1) in many cases, both spouses work in the business out of necessity or desire, and (2) whether your spouse works in your business or not, he or she is an integral part of your personal "inside" team. Your spouse or significant other is probably the biggest influence on your success. If your spouse is in your corner, you can do the things needed to build your business.

If there's conflict or tension, however, you're going to have problems in both the business and the relationship. Building a business is a relationship stressor. It's no accident that the majority of entrepreneurs have been divorced at least once. Conversely, when your spouse or significant other supports your efforts with the business, you can put your energy into it with a clear head and happy heart.

Just remember what I said in the chapter on your life blueprint: no matter how hard it is to make the time, you must give your spouse/significant other the attention he or she needs. You neglect this vital relationship at your peril because you will never have a small business and big life without the support and understanding of the person most important to you.

The rest of your outside team includes all the different professionals and companies you deal with in your business. Bankers, insurance agents, attorneys, accountants, marketers, consultants, delivery services, suppliers, utilities—there are many individuals and companies that help you stay in business every single day. As a business owner, in the same way that you create strong relationships with your inside team, you and your employees must create, build, and maintain good relationships with your outside team.

Some business books speak of these outside team members as being your "customers" just as much as the people who buy your products or use your services. I prefer to think of them as a part of the team that supports a business. I want to treat them well and also to use their unique gifts to help my business and my inside team to succeed.

There's a saying in Spanish that translates as, "Tell me who you associate with and I'll tell you who you are." There's a temptation as a business owner to hire both inside and outside team members based on familiarity rather than skill or ability. You ask your personal attorney if he can handle your business law needs. You talk to your tax preparer about doing your company books. You happen to know that the mother of one of your daughter's friends does a little writing on the side, so you ask her if she can write copy for your Web site. Maybe you even have your fourteen-year-old son build your Web site for you.

I'm not saying that all of these people won't do a good job—but will they do the *best* job? Do they have the knowledge, ability, skill, and habits to produce the outstanding results you want?

Your business support team is designed to take your business to the next level of success. This team should be composed of people who, like you, are expressing their unique abilities in their professions. If they are great at what they do, they can help you become great as well.

How much better will your business be if you have an accountant who can help you save money on taxes, show you ways to maximize your cash flow, help minimize outstanding receivables, and guide you in planning properly for the future? How much safer will you feel knowing that your insurance agent specializes in your kind of business and can recommend policies that cover you for both major and minor problems? How much more efficient can you be with a bank that helps you roll over extra profits into interest-bearing accounts, and contacts you if they can get you a better rate on your current business loan?

There are hundreds of thousands of professionals who can support you in building your small business. You need to (1) identify your current and future needs, and then (2) hire the people who can help you with both. You may spend more money than you would like for their time and expertise, because these professionals usually have had years of training and experience in their fields, but as long as you find ethical, qualified professionals, it will be some of the best money you can invest. You don't necessarily need to hire the most expensive people, as long as they are good people with the right education, experience, credentials, and integrity.

How do you find these professionals? Recommendations from people you know are always valuable, but I would suggest you research any attorney, accountant, or other professional with the professional associations in your area. Check attorneys with the state and local bar associations, CPAs with the American Institute of Certified Public Accountants (www.aicpa.org), and financial planners with the Financial Planning Association (www.fpanet.org). Always ask for references, and check them. Any reputable professional should be glad to have you contact past or current clients to ask about their services.

Finally, make sure you know and understand the fee structure of your outside specialists. Many of them will charge an hourly rate and bill you for expenses on top of that. Especially when you're first starting out and money is tight, it's vital to be able to estimate the costs of these critical services and put them into your budget. To get an accurate estimate, make sure you are very specific about what you are asking the professional to do. Filing a quarterly tax return will cost far less than doing your business's year-end financial statements, for instance, yet they both fall into the category of accounting services. The more specific you are in your requests, the better.

There are five categories of experts you should consider hiring.

- *An attorney.* You will need someone who specializes in business issues. Attorneys nowadays specialize in everything from tax law to intellectual property to patents and more. There also are attorneys whose clients are mostly small business owners. Choose the attorney or law firm that provides services most appropriate to your primary needs.

- *An accountant/bookkeeper* and a *tax preparer.* Sometimes this person is one and the same; other times you can have a bookkeeper, a certified public accountant, and a tax preparer, depending on the accounting professional's skills and your own needs. Accounting and bookkeeping are some of the most underappreciated professions, and most accountants are honest, ethical, and professional. A good accountant and tax preparer can save you a great deal of money and take a lot of hassle off your back.

  Most business owners like to work with CPAs (certified public accountants); just make sure to ask any candidate about his or her experience in working with companies like yours and the kind of accounting you use (accrual or cash). I also suggest that your tax preparer be an enrolled agent (EA)—someone who is licensed by the IRS to prepare taxes and represent you at any audit. Again, check references on any professional you plan to utilize.

- *A property and casualty insurance agent.* You will need insurance for your employees (workers' compensation insurance), property and liability insurance for you, assets, errors, and omissions insurance or professional liability insurance, and more. A relationship with a good insurance agent who specializes in small business can be a blessing if you ever have to use one of your policies. Look for someone who has a CLU (Chartered Life Underwriter) designation. And make sure to update your policies regularly.

  Anyone who has had the misfortune to be in a major disaster, such as Hurricane Katrina in 2005 or the big earthquake in Northridge, California, in 1994, knows that keeping your coverage up to date and knowing exactly what's covered and what isn't can make the difference between closing down permanently and being able to reopen your doors with a minimum loss.

- *A business banker.* A lot of first-time entrepreneurs think of the Small Business Administration (SBA) when it comes to business loans. However, the SBA doesn't actually loan you money—they simply guarantee the loan you receive from a bank. Plus, you have to be in business for three years before you can even apply for an SBA loan. That's why a good business banker can be one of the most important team members you can have. A business banker can provide you with the working capital to get your business started, to keep it going, or to expand its operations. You can purchase commercial property, equipment, software, or get operating capital, depending on your individual needs.

The best place to find a business banker is where you already have a banking relationship—that is, the bank where you have your personal accounts. Ask to see the business banking specialist at your branch. The key to getting help with your small business is to do everything you can before you actually need the money. Get to know the people at the local branch where you do your banking, including the business banking specialist. Getting acquainted with all these people before you go in to request a loan will make the process smoother for both you and them.

When you first start a business, most banks will be looking at your personal banking record and credit scores to see if you'll be a good financial risk. If you handle your personal money well, then you are more likely to handle a business's money well. So make sure your personal accounts are in order. Know your credit rating (you can get free copies of your credit reports once a year from www.annualcredit report.com) and do whatever you can to raise them. Have your personal financial statements in order.

If you already have a business and are looking to expand, make sure that your accounts are in order and you are not trying to conceal income. When you work with a good CPA and bookkeeper and you're able to provide your bank with detailed financial statements and tax returns, you are more likely to receive bigger loans at better rates.

Remember, bankers want to lend money to people who will be good clients and pay the loans back on time. A good business banker can help you package your loan and walk you through the entire process. Based on your business financial statements and your credit rating, many banks will give you a start-up loan. Once you've established the relationship, and with a good credit record, getting a loan can be as easy as filling out an application.

When I opened my business in Santa Fe Springs, California, I needed to get all new equipment (computers, printers, fax machines, software, and so on). My business banker told me, "You need a loan? We can give you $35,000 immediately." They even filled out the application for me; all I had to do was go to the bank and sign the paperwork. Because I was a long-term customer in good standing, the bank was happy to loan me money without any fuss.

• *A financial planner.* Of course, as a Certified Financial Planner myself, I believe this person is an absolutely essential member of your team. A financial planner can help you create a better future by helping you (1) plan for growth, (2) handle potential financial challenges, and (3) create long-term goals for yourself and your business. Find someone who specializes in the needs of small business owners.

Please note that I said you need a financial planner, not a financial consultant or an investment salesperson. Your stockbroker or someone who works at your bank may or may not have the expertise or experience you need. Look for a person who has at least a CFP® designation; this means they have received advanced training in financial planning.

If you are going to get any investment advice to go along with financial planning, make sure that your advisor is also a Registered Investment Advisor, who is registered with and reviewed by the SEC or your state's regulatory body.

THE PROOF OF A GREAT TEAM
IS IN ITS EXECUTION

Have you ever watched a truly great sports team? Everyone is in the right position, using his or her unique talents and abilities. The team is working together toward the common goal of winning. The players support each other; each person is just as happy when a teammate scores a goal or makes a great save as when the player does it himself or herself. The players look up to the coach, listen to him or her, and respect what he or she has to say.

There's energy around a great team—excitement, happiness, a sense of power. Such a team is willing to go the extra mile, spend the extra time practicing, and do whatever it takes to prevail. Just by seeing them walk on the field, you know they will accomplish great things.

On the other hand, have you ever seen a team that looks as if it has everything in place but somehow they aren't quite together? How many times have you witnessed an almost-great football team take the ball down to the one-yard line but not make the touchdown? Or the soccer team that creates more opportunities to score than their opponents but somehow fails to put the ball into the net?

A successful team requires *execution*. The team must have enough motivation as a group to produce the results even when the going is tough. In your business, your team must know the "why" of your company and believe in your mission. Like a sports team, these people must keep their eyes on the ball and not get bogged down in the day-to-day minutia of getting the job done.

You, as team coach (owner), must help your players (employees) utilize their unique talents to executing the plays (fulfilling the functions on your business blueprint) until you win the game. In the case of your business, however, the game is ongoing. It's something you win quarter by quarter, year by year.

NINE WAYS TO SUPPORT YOUR TEAM

As owner/coach, you are ultimately responsible for the success or failure of your team. You can support your team in nine different ways.

1. *Keep your employees' eyes on the prize.* Make sure they know your vision for the company and that they believe in the vision almost as much as you do. When people are emotionally involved, they will give their best efforts.

2. *Link their personal goals and dreams to their accomplishments at work.* People work better and are happier in their jobs when they feel personally involved in what they are doing.

3. *Make sure your people are in the right jobs for their knowledge, abilities, skills, and habits.* You don't want a quarterback to waste his time tackling, or a kicker to have to run with the ball. Your employees will work better and be happier if their jobs allow them to do what they are good at and what they love to do. If you need someone to fill a function and your current employees are not suited to handle it, you can either (a) train someone who has that ability, (b) hire someone new, or (c) contract with an outside firm to do the work.

4. *Use your business blueprint to help your employees be absolutely clear about the functions you are expecting them to handle.* No one, including you, can do it all. That's why you build a strong team—so no one will have to do too much. When your employees are absolutely clear about what their jobs are and what functions are their responsibilities, they will do a better job, not just individually, but also as part of a well-functioning team. There will be less duplication of effort and better use of everyone's time and resources.

5. *Put systems in place to automate the business functions.* You can think of your systems as being like the plays in a football game. When the quarterback (or the coach on the sidelines) calls for a particular play, everyone on the team knows what he or she is supposed to do. In the same way, your business systems will help your employees know how to handle the functions for which they are responsible. Systems will make your employees' jobs easier (and help you sleep better at night).

6. *Delegate, don't abdicate.* Check in frequently with your employees to confirm the job is being done and they have the wherewithal to accomplish what you are asking of them. Checking should not be micromanaging; it should be more like supporting your team in being its best. It's confirming that everyone knows what to do and has everything they need to do it.

7. *Praise frequently as you support high standards throughout the team.* Recognizing people's efforts consistently is an enormous motivator. We all want to know we're doing a good job and that others see the efforts we're making. Saying "Thank you" and "Well done!" when warranted is one of the most important actions an owner can take.

   You also must hold your team to a high standard. A team is only as strong as its weakest member, and often the weakest member is most in need of your support. If certain employees are not pulling their weight, first check to make sure you have done the six things listed earlier. Are those employees enrolled in the company vision? Are they emotionally involved in their work? Is the job utilizing their K.A.S.H.? Are they clear on the functions they're expected to handle? Do they feel they're being micromanaged or ignored? Have you supported them so they have the tools they need to do their job well? Have you praised them for what they have done right while keeping them to a high standard? You may find that doing all these things will strengthen your "weak links" and help them become, if not high performers, at least solid players on the team.

   Of course, there are certain things that will cause you to terminate someone's employment immediately. If this happens, do so cleanly, clearly, and firmly. Once they have left, make sure you tell your team. You don't necessarily need to share the specifics, but let them know the general circumstances. It's better to be clear yet compassionate than to allow the rumor mill to create fear and uncertainty in your team.

8. *Create a healthy emotional environment in your business.* Tension in the office between coworkers, stress around a project with a deadline, and

financial challenges can have a negative impact on even a world-class team. In my first business, when my partner and I had different visions for our company, it created problems. Our employees started to feel like a dysfunctional family: employees would go to my partner and get one answer, and if they did not like it they would come to me, hoping for a different answer. We started to see backstabbing, people talking behind other people's backs, not trusting each other. We realized the only way to be successful and stay competitive was to have healthy employees, and this required a change in our leadership.

Whatever the issue is in your business, you owe it to yourself and your employees to handle things immediately. If an ongoing situation is out of your control (conditions in the marketplace change, someone on the team has left unexpectedly, the bank has pulled your financing), your first responsibility is to be honest with your team. There's nothing worse than a workplace where rumors are running rampant but no one has accurate information. It creates fear, misunderstanding, distrust, and a lot of other very negative emotions. Have an all-company meeting and give people the facts. Let them know what you are doing to handle the situation and what they can do to help. You do not have to be a "cock-eyed optimist" and try to make things seem hunky-dory. Simply being honest will go a long way toward bringing your team together.

Most of the time, creating a healthy emotional environment in your team is easy. You do it by caring for your team members, respecting their abilities, asking about their lives, and doing the little things that enhance every relationship. You also create a healthy emotional environment by fulfilling your own responsibilities in the company.

Every team needs a coach and a leader. Without one, conflicts and power struggles can arise. In the same way that you need to be a parent to your kids instead of being their "friend," you need to be the coach of your team and the owner of your business instead of just another team player. While you relate to your employees as friends, too, let them know that you also believe the buck stops with you, that you are the one ultimately responsible for the success or failure of the business. They will respect you for it.

9. *Lead by example.* Someone once said you can't teach what you haven't done or don't know. In the same way, you cannot lead people to be a great team unless you embody the same qualities you're asking them to demonstrate. You must do your job as well as you want them to do theirs. Your own standards have to be as high as, if not higher than, the ones you're asking them to meet.

I'm sure you have heard the expression, "You must walk your talk." If your employees are burning the midnight oil to get a project out the door, how are they going to feel if you're out on the town with your spouse while they're hard at work? I'm not saying that you have to be there every time someone works late in your business, but your employees need to feel you are setting the right example for them in the way you work and live.

The bigger the dream, the better the team needed to create it. All entrepreneurs start with a dream of creating a business where there was none before. Recruiting and building a team to turn that dream into a reality not only will make the dream possible, it also will make the journey to your dream more enjoyable along the way. Sharing a dream is far more exciting than creating it on your own. And I think you'll find that building a team to co-create your dream will allow your business to expand beyond your wildest imaginings.

11

Conclusion: Living the Dash

L et's take another look at the five steps of building a small business, big life:

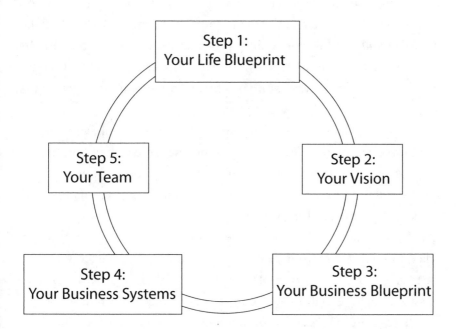

The steps to creating a small business, big life are part of an endless circle. Your life blueprint sets the priorities for your life. As a business owner, you will put what you do in your business into the context of your life's priorities. Your business blueprint gives those priorities concrete form, in the plan for a business that will create the life you desire. Your business systems will enable you to turn your idea for a business into a day-to-day operation. And finally, putting together your team will make it possible to transform the dream of your business into reality. But every step leads you back to your life blueprint. If your small business is not leading you to the life you desire, then you must go back, reevaluate, retool, and revise.

I'm not saying that every day in your business is going to be the way you want it. In fact, every day in your business will undoubtedly bring you frustrations and joys, challenges and solutions, defeats and victories. Some days you will come home at midnight, thinking, *Why in the world did I ever believe I could make a go of this?* You'll have times when your spouse wonders if you still care about your family, when you feel guilty for missing your child's baseball game or piano recital, or when you work another weekend instead of going to the neighborhood barbecue. Other days you will feel like you're on top of the world—when your first big order or client comes in, when your team finishes a project and sends it out the door, when you pay off your first business loan or buy your first store.

My hope is that with what you've learned in this book, you will also experience the quiet pleasure of closing the office door on a Friday evening knowing that you and your team have worked well, produced great results, enjoyed each other's company, and added yet another little brick to the foundation of a small business and big life for all concerned. On those Fridays, you will go home to spend time with your family, to relax, to take care of your health, to put your time and energy into the parts of your life blueprint that your small business exists to make possible. I believe that if you use the five steps outlined in this book, you will have more of those happy moments to counterbalance the tough times. You will have created a strong foundation that will keep your small business healthy and prosperous.

USING THE FIVE STEPS
TO DEAL WITH CHANGE

Life and business are always changing. As a business owner you must be ready to adapt to changing circumstances and take advantage of the new business climate. Business is Darwinian: it works on the "survival of the fittest" model, and the key to survival is adaptability. One of the greatest strengths of the five steps is the way in which they allow your small business to adapt quickly to change.

Let's say you own a small printing shop in your town, producing business cards, brochures, flyers, signage, and so on. You have five employees, including your spouse who works in the office. One day you're walking down the street and you notice a sign on a building a block away: "FASTSIGNS Opening Here in One Month!" A FASTSIGNS franchise is opening a store in your town. FASTSIGNS does a lot of the same things as your business. Over the next few days several of your customers call to tell you they have received letters from the owner of FASTSIGNS, listing rates that are below what you've been charging for signage and printing.

Many small business owners at this point would be very worried and unsure of what to do next. However, you go straight back to the vision for your business, which was to be a one-stop shop providing quality printing support for local businesses. You take a look at your vision and ask, "Do I need to change this to fit these new circumstances?" and you decide to change the word *printing*. Your new vision is to be a one-stop shop providing quality *business* support to the local community.

With that vision, you review your business blueprint. In the past you focused on printing services, and at the request of your customers you expanded into signage. What other services could you offer that would provide quality business support? "What if we could not only print brochures but also mail them to local customers?" you ask yourself. "Or perhaps we could turn a company's brochure into a Web site or at least upload the brochure content into the current company Web site. Do we have anyone on our team who has those skills and abilities or could learn them?"

You bring your team together and propose your ideas for a change in vision and added services. You discover that Ron, a young man who runs one of the presses, studied design in college, and his roommate, Thomas, does freelance Web site design. Your spouse does some research and shows you a simple fulfillment computer program that will link to your printing press and print mailing labels directly onto brochures.

You retool the functions on your business blueprint, putting your spouse in charge of fulfillment and Ron in charge of design. You hire Thomas on a freelance basis, with a promise of full-time work as the business expands. You and your team work on creating the systems that will support the increased workload. Because you involve your entire team, you can get most of the new plan in place within just a few weeks.

The week before FASTSIGNS is scheduled to open, you drop by the store and ask to see the owner. You welcome her to the neighborhood and give her a copy of your new brochure describing your expanded offerings. "I imagine you'll have some clients who will need additional services for their businesses," you say. "I'll be happy to refer clients who need signs to you. I'd appreciate if you would keep us in mind if you have clients who need the kinds of services we offer. This community is expanding, and there's plenty of business for both of us. I'd love to see us both succeed."

Instead of throwing you into a panic and driving you out of business, the advent of a new "competitor" allows you to refine your vision of your business and create something even greater. Your team is using even more of their K.A.S.H. (knowledge, abilities, skills, and habits), and they are excited about the possibilities. You have redesigned your blueprint and created the systems to handle your expanded workload.

All of this happened because you used the five steps to build a small business effectively. Instead of reacting to events, you responded to them, and your results reflect your actions.

That's the beauty of the five steps to build a small business. They give you a path to follow in good times and rough times. They will allow you to handle the inevitable changes of life and business with far more ease and better results. And they will give you much more clarity and greater peace of mind than you might think possible for a small business owner.

MEASURE REGULARLY, IMPROVE INCREMENTALLY

Change is not the only challenge most businesses face. Simply managing to stay in business is usually the first obstacle. It's all very well and good setting up a blueprint, creating systems, and putting together a team; now you have to get in the trenches and do the daily work of putting out product and bringing in revenues. Certainly following the five steps will make the day-to-day easier, but there's one more thing you must do to make sure you're on track: you must measure your results.

The only way for a business to improve and grow is to check your progress consistently against the goals you have set for it. The same is true for your life. The only way to know how you're progressing is to schedule regular, periodic evaluations of both your business and your life.

W. Edwards Deming was the father of the modern quality control movement. He went to Japan after World War II and learned that constant small changes were the secret to large improvements over time. He also learned that the best way to know how you're doing is to measure your results frequently and consistently. You, too, must evaluate your progress by measuring your results frequently and consistently.

As I heard in an Anthony Robbins course many years ago, most people measure their results once a year on December 31, when they look at their New Year's resolutions for the first time since they made them 364 days earlier. How often do most businesses measure results? Quarterly, perhaps—maybe monthly. You should measure your business results at least weekly, and depending on the business, you should check in daily.

Some measures of progress are easy to obtain and assess. In addition to your weekly measurements, each quarter you should review your business blueprint, systems, and team to see what, if any, adjustments need to be made. Do some of your business functions need to be updated, delegated, or switched from one employee to another? Should any revisions be made to your systems? Are there changes to your team that need to be reflected on your business blueprint? Have you hired employees or outside contractors? Are there new functions that have been added to your business blueprint that must be allocated to someone (preferably someone other than you the owner)?

I suggest that these quarterly reviews happen off-site and involve as many of your employees as possible. You would be surprised at the number of great ideas and fresh perspectives that your employees can bring to reviewing and revising your business blueprint and systems.

You also will create a stronger team by asking for their input and then implementing the ideas that fit within the overall vision for the company. Take advantage of your employees' knowledge and enthusiasm, and you will increase both.

As the owner, you, too, need to spend time measuring your company's progress and evaluating the "big picture" results of your vision. You should spend at least a few hours each quarter by yourself, reviewing your vision for the business.

How is your current enterprise fulfilling that vision? Does the business need to change to meet your vision, or do you need to alter the vision slightly to fit the ways in which the business is evolving? A small business has a life of its own, and like most living beings it does not always follow even the best-laid plans and visions. By reassociating yourself to the vision for your business, you can more easily determine whether your vision or your business needs to change in order to produce the small business, big life you desire.

Remember, however, that your small business is only part of the big picture of your life. Just as you review your business results, it's even more essential to review your personal results based on your life blueprint. Every three months, you should take a look at your blueprint and rate yourself on a scale of 1 to 10 on your values, life focus areas, and roles. Where are you making progress? Where are you falling behind? What areas do you need to bring to the forefront for a while so you can restore balance to your life? Remember Deming's premise: the only way we get better is to measure consistently.

Measuring should not be an occasion to beat yourself up, but an honest assessment of what's working and what's not working yet. In many cases, upgrading your score in any given area is relatively simple. If your health has slipped in the last quarter, how can you plan to get to the gym three times a week? If your finances need attention, can you make an appointment with a personal financial planner? Maybe you have spent more time focusing on your role as a parent, and your role as a spouse has suffered. What could you do to give your spouse a "jackpot" that would make him or her feel completely loved?

The key to improvement is measurement: catch problems while they are small so you can fix them quickly, rather than waiting until things fall apart. Both in terms of your business and your life, consistent measurement and improvement will make achieving a small business and big life much easier.

Measuring regularly also helps you step out of the stream of day-to-day business and life so that you can focus on what's truly important. Everyone gets caught up in dealing with emergencies, deadlines, and issues. It's easy to let events pull you so far off course that eventually you end up at a destination that's miles away from your original goal.

As the leader of your business, it's your responsibility to maintain the focus on your vision and steer the "ship" of your business unfailingly toward its true north. Every time you or your employees measure, you are checking your results against your goals. It's a great reminder of what you must always keep in mind: the achievement of your vision.

Your measurements in business and life should assess more than the concrete results of revenues, sales, growth, and systems. You also need to measure more intangible things like satisfaction, fulfillment, eagerness to get at the day, and happiness when you leave work at night. If your team or you are feeling discontented or unhappy, that may be a sign that either (1) things are off track, or (2) your results are not fulfilling your vision for life and/or business.

Of course, everyone can have a bad day, and there are also events that can momentarily produce feelings of unhappiness no matter what. If you remember our personal responsibility formula back in chapter 3, the goal always must be to respond to events rather than react to them so that you can produce the outcomes you desire. But prolonged negative emotions are a sign that you need to make a change.

If you are unhappy because things are off track in your business, what can you do to get back on course? Are your systems in need of adjustment? Are certain functions not being handled in the proper ways? Are there problems with your team? Do you need to adjust your blueprint, systems, or team in response to changes in circumstances? Or do you simply need to take a few moments to remember why you're doing this?

I have a friend who has been in business for a number of years, and he has created quite a bit of success for himself and his company. Every time I see him he is always upbeat and excited about what he is doing with his business. I asked him recently how he has stayed so motivated through the years. "Two reasons," he told me. "I have a picture of my wife and children on my desk, and every morning I look at them and remember why I work so hard. I also look at their photo as I'm getting ready to leave at night, and I get excited about going home to spend time with the most important people in my life.

"The second reason is sharing my success with others," he continued. "We have profit sharing here, so all the employees participate in our success. We also contribute a great deal to charity. Every year I set a goal for myself of giving a certain percentage of my income to my church, my kids' school, and the local community clinic. My employees also participate in United Way, and we all help out with the local food bank at Thanksgiving.

"Every month at our employee meeting we not only talk about our revenues and accomplishments, we also talk about the people we have helped and what we are planning to do as a group in the next quarter to make a difference. Whenever I look at our financial statements and see the bottom line, I think of all the things that money is going to allow us to do to make our lives and the lives of a lot of other people much better. That's a lot more exciting to me than just seeing a bigger number at the end of the year."

My friend had stumbled onto the real secret of a small business, big life: a focus on something bigger than yourself or your business. Is your bottom line important? Of course. But why? Is it so you can buy a bigger house or send your kids to a better school? It's nice to be able to live a more abundant lifestyle. But ultimately what will give you the greatest satisfaction and fulfillment isn't the car you drive or the fact that your kid went to Harvard and you live in the big house at the top of the hill.

Even being the most successful businessperson in your community will give you limited happiness—unless you are happy with who you are and what you have done to achieve your success. The relationships you create and the contributions you make to others are the truest measures of success.

FOCUS ON WHAT IS TRULY IMPORTANT

Not long ago, Angie and I went to the funeral of the father of one of our friends. The man had lived a good, long life, and there were a lot of people who came to the cemetery to honor him. After the ceremony, Angie and I strolled down the way, looking at the graves. Some of the graves looked well tended, with fresh flowers or small flags. Others looked as if no one had visited in a very long time.

I nudged Angie. "Look at the inscriptions on the headstones," I said. "'Beloved husband and father,' 'Wife, mother, and friend,' 'He gave his life for his country.' Do you notice something? Not one headstone says, 'A great businessperson,' or 'She always made a profit,' or 'He owned twelve stores.' That's not what people are remembered for."

"I also noticed something," Angie said. "Most of the headstones have at least a name, a birth date, and date of death, with a dash in between the dates. Do you realize that a person's entire life is represented by that dash?"

We all start in one place—our mother's womb—and we are all going to end up in the same place—six feet under. You are not going to take anything with you. When it comes time for you to be carted off to the cemetery, your hearse won't be followed by a car filled with money or a truck towing your office building or restaurant. We are all heading for the same destination; what is important is the journey. You are living the "dash"— your journey of life—every day, and how you live it will determine how happy you are and the quality of the legacy you leave behind far more than what's in your bank account or how big your business has become.

Focusing on what's important is remembering that your business must be part of your life, not the other way around. You may decide you want to grow your business to be a multibillion-dollar enterprise with branches in fifty countries. If that's your goal, great. But I'm more interested in making sure that whether you have one branch or one hundred, your life is rich in things other than money.

You might be more fulfilled with one storefront in East Los Angeles with ten employees. A business that runs well, is fun to own, and allows you to make the most of your unique abilities is important. If your business creates good money for you and your employees so that you can take care of yourselves and contribute to others, if your business gives your family a comfortable life and also permits you to spend time with your family creating memories and relationships that they will treasure long after you've gone, then you have made a success of your business and your life.

True greatness resides not in the success of our businesses but in the success of our lives. So how do you want to live? If you're one of the thousands of people who want more than your current level of financial abundance, if you see a small business as a way to support your family while you utilize more of your own talents and abilities, my hope is that this book has given you some of the tools you need to create a small business that will give you the big life of your dreams.

Dreams are essential. Having the tools to create dreams will open the door to success. To walk through the door, however, takes both inspiration and perspiration (to paraphrase Thomas Edison). It takes vision and action, persistence and consistency, and above all, belief in a better future for yourself and the people you love.

One morning while I was getting dressed, the television in our bedroom was on. I heard a news report about a young Latina who had received an award from the Los Angeles Chamber of Commerce, so I sat down to watch. This young girl, about eleven or twelve years old, had won the state championship for the best violinist for her age group.

At the awards ceremony, they told a little of her story. Her family was so poor that they could not afford to buy her a violin. The school was in a tough neighborhood, and they would not allow the kids to take the instruments home because all too often the children would be beaten up and the instruments would be stolen and then sold.

One of the presenters asked the little girl, "How did you become so good?"

She answered, "At night my mom would turn out the light so I'd have to go to sleep. Instead of sleeping, I'd practice the violin in my head."

After they gave her the award (a big glass plaque), someone stepped onstage, holding a violin case. He opened the case, gave the violin to the girl, and said, "This is for you—you finally have your very own violin. Now, won't you play something for us?"

You should have seen her face! She put the violin under her chin and started playing, and the camera focused on the girl's parents. Tears were running down their cheeks—tears of joy and pride in what their child had accomplished.

That young girl exemplifies what you really need in order to create a small business and a big life. You need to have a dream so big and so important to you that nothing—no person, no circumstance—will stand in your way. You need to seek out and make use of any and all the resources available to you. You have to be willing to put in the work, day after day, with little or no visible progress or reward, knowing that you are moving toward your goal. You must overcome obstacles by being creative and persistent. And you must know that your goal will not just raise you up, but it will also elevate and inspire others to help you and to be on your team.

I wish you great things as you create your own small business. May your journey to financial greatness be rich in wonder, excitement, passion, teamwork, growth, and, above all, love. May you be an inspiration to others. May your life be rich in what truly matters—in the relationships you build and the difference you make in the world. Then you will truly have lived a *big* life!

Guideposts for
Your Journey

Growth Process Chart: Clarify, Create, Commit, Complete

All business—indeed, all life—consists of setting goals, working toward their attainment, and then setting newer, higher goals. I believe there is a cycle that individuals and businesses follow in the growth process. I created the chart on page 177 to make the process of business planning and execution as simple as possible. This is the foundation of all the business consulting I do. You can use these same steps when it comes to creating and implementing the life and business blueprints that I outlined in part 2.

Suppose you come to see me to upgrade your business. Once you have created your life blueprint (chapter 6) and you have defined your vision for your business (chapter 7), you are ready to set goals using these four steps.

I. CLARIFY

To make a goal achievable, you must clarify exactly what it means and why it's important to you. We use the Values, Roles, and Life Focus charts you completed as part of your life blueprint as the basis for deciding what's most important for your life and your business. (See chapter 6 for these charts.) Based on that, you will choose a goal and make it as specific as possible.

2. CREATE

A goal without a plan is nothing more than wishful thinking. The plan for your small business is the business blueprint and systems you created in chapters 8 and 9.

3. COMMIT

Now that you have a goal and a plan, you need to commit to doing the daily follow-through that will make your dream a reality. Review the first two steps (Clarify and Create) to make sure you have not missed anything and to identify any potential obstacles that might show up so you can handle them in advance. Then you must work on becoming fully committed to your goal and inspired by its accomplishment. Motivation is temporary. It will get you to the office, but it won't lead you to make any extra effort. Inspiration will get you up each and every morning, excited about what you can accomplish. Inspiration is the emotion that will carry you through the tough times, keep you creative and upbeat when obstacles appear, and keep your team on track and eager to work with you as you turn your vision into action.

4. COMPLETE

Finally, you must create practical systems to make sure you can complete your goals. I once heard that "to make something powerful, you need to make it practical." In this step you set up systems to monitor your goals to make sure you are staying on track. Part of the systems you created in chapter 9 can help you complete your goals.

The by-product of completing all four steps is Confidence, which gives you the Courage to think about new or bigger goals. As you see below, this growth process is an upward spiral. Each success carries you to a higher level of achievement as you turn your dreams and goals into stepping-stones to the business and life you desire.

Enjoy the process!

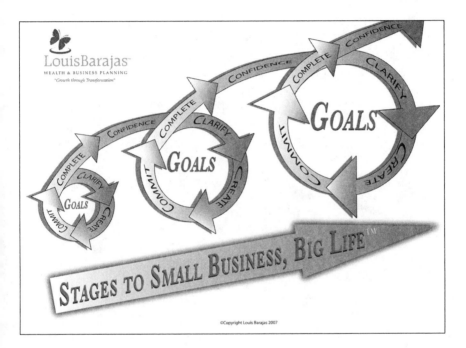

The 22 Temptations
of a Small Business Owner

I n my years of working with small business owners, I found that there are
many temptations that can pull entrepreneurs off track and cause them
to fail. (I've also been guilty of a few of them myself.) Now I give this list to
my clients right up front. I tell them to put the list in their day planners and
on the wall by their computers. I suggest you do the same. Avoid these mistakes and you'll increase your chances of success a thousand percent.

1. TEMPTED TO START A BUSINESS JUST BECAUSE YOU
KNOW HOW TO DO SOMETHING (CREATE JEWELRY,
BAKE A BETTER PIE, ETC.)

Just because you are good at doing something does not mean that you
know how to run a business that does that same thing. If you followed that
logic, there would be a million Martha Stewarts and Marie Callenders! You
need to learn all the facets of running a business before you put your time,
capital, and resources on the line. Part 2 of this book should help you learn
the skills you need to run a business whose product or service is something
you're good at doing or creating. Pay particular attention to chapter 8 on
creating your business blueprint.

2. TEMPTED TO START A BUSINESS WITHOUT A BUSINESS PLAN AND WITHOUT LIFE AND BUSINESS BLUEPRINTS

I never said you did not need a business plan; what I said was that you need a life blueprint and a business blueprint to create a successful small business, big life. If you are going to need financing, especially from the Small Business Administration, you are going to need a business plan. Go to www.sba.gov for a business plan template.

3. TEMPTED NOT TO BEGIN WITH THE END IN MIND

You have to see your business up and running before you apply for a loan or rent a storefront or print a business card. You have to start with complete clarity as to exactly what your business will look like. It's almost like a light you're heading toward as you walk the path of business creation. Vision and visualization are key skills for any business owner. See chapter 7 to learn more about creating a strong vision for your business.

You also need to create a plan and a vision for eventually getting out of your business (see Temptation 22). Everyone retires at some point. You need to plan for your graceful exit so your business will provide you with either retirement income or a nice nest egg to invest in your next enterprise.

4. TEMPTED TO WORK LONGER AND HARDER TO OVERCOME BUSINESS CHALLENGES

Business is a challenge when you are just starting out, and when things get tough, human nature will tell you to work harder. However, working even harder than you already are usually is the recipe for burnout. When I was learning to play golf, I would swing as hard as I could to try to hit the ball a long way. I learned rather quickly that swinging hard will not get the ball any farther down the fairway. I needed to be relaxed to play well. The same thing is true in a business. When I have a client who is frustrated and burned out, I *make* him or her take time off. This can be a struggle, especially since often the client is burnt out because the business isn't doing well! However, it's uncanny how a fresh and relaxed perspective can increase your efficiency and effectiveness in running your small business.

5. TEMPTED TO HIRE PEOPLE WHOM YOU LIKE AND WHO ARE EXACTLY LIKE YOU

When you build your business blueprint, you will become aware of all the major functions required to run your business. Some of those functions will need talent and skills that are different from yours. If you hire people with similar aptitudes and personality, you will not build a strong company. For example, if you are more of an idea or "big picture" person, you will do yourself a disservice if you hire an accountant with the same attributes. Good accountants have the opposite traits: they should be very focused and detailed. You must hire the correct person with the natural innate talents for the major core functions of your business. As discussed in chapter 10, to get an accurate picture of potential employees' strengths and weaknesses, use personality and skills tests before you hire people. You also might want to read *Now, Discover Your Strengths* to learn more about building a great team of individuals with complementary strengths.

6. TEMPTED TO BRING IN UNNECESSARY PARTNERS

Sometimes, mostly because of fear of doing it alone or because of lack of money, small business owners bring in unnecessary partners. Bringing in a business partner can be tougher than a marriage, and getting the partner out of the business can be worse than a divorce. The biggest problem with business partners is determining whether they share your vision of the business or if they have their own vision. Most businesses require only one visionary; otherwise you end up like a car with two drivers, with nobody going anywhere and lots of fights about who gets to steer. Before you bring in a partner, see if you can hire the person or barter for his or her services. You will probably be happier in the long run. If you do bring in a partner, make sure the terms of your partner's involvement in the business are clarified, and put those terms in writing before the deal is signed. Consider it a "prenup" for your business life.

7. TEMPTED TO CONTROL EVERYTHING

If you feel that you always need to be at your business or be in charge of everything, you will set yourself up for burnout and eventual failure in your business and personal life. As small business author Michael Gerber taught me, if you have to be at your business all the time, you don't own a business: you own a job. If you do not develop your business systems and delegate the work, you will never own a business. It's as simple as that. Go back to chapter 9 and make sure you have the systems in place to support your having both a business and a life.

8. TEMPTED TO BE EVERYTHING TO EVERYBODY

Bill Cosby once said, "I don't know the key to success, but I do know the key to failure, and that is to be everything to everyone." You need to identify what kind of service or product you want to have and then market it to the ideal client who would use your services. If you try to sell expensive products to poor people, you will fail. Focus on the type of service or product you want to sell, and then try to identify where you are going to find your clients.

9. TEMPTED TO STRENGTHEN YOUR WEAKNESSES

Every study shows that if you focus on your weaknesses all you will have are stronger weaknesses. You need to focus on and continuously strengthen your unique God-given talents. Don't try to cure your weaknesses; it's easier to delegate or manage them while you focus instead on making your talents bloom.

A lot of my clients have a hard time identifying or articulating their unique strengths. If this is you, try doing the following: (a) Write a letter or have a conversation with close friends, colleagues, or family members and ask them what they think makes you unique. If they had to come to you for one of your strengths, what would they come to you for? (b) Read *Now, Discover Your Strengths* and take the authors' online strengths finder test.

10. TEMPTED NOT TO SPEND MONEY (INVEST) IN YOUR BUSINESS UNTIL YOU MAKE MORE MONEY FIRST

This is the big catch-22. In my first year of business I made just enough money to keep the doors open. Then my phone started ringing, but I just could not see clients and answer phones at the same time. I knew I needed to hire a receptionist, but how could I hire a receptionist if I was only making enough money to pay my bills? I asked myself what I would tell clients if they had a similar problem—and I hired a receptionist. In the beginning I had to pay her wages through my credit card, but in the first year of her employment I made a lot more money. I was able to cover her salary and pay myself decent wages. Sometimes you will need to spend, or as I like to call it, *invest,* money on things that will create a positive impact on your bottom line.

11. TEMPTED TO PROMOTE EMPLOYEES TO LEVELS OF INCOMPETENCE

This is one of the biggest mistakes owners make. Just because you have employees who know how to do something doesn't mean that they should be promoted to supervisory or managerial roles if they can't manage others. Remember that most of the greatest athletes rarely ever make great coaches. Great managers have different, unique abilities. Make sure the people you hire to manage others are great at managing people.

12. TEMPTED TO GROW YOUR BUSINESS WITHOUT BUSINESS SYSTEMS

Good systems are your business foundation. If you run into difficulties in your business, 99 percent of the time a good system is the solution. Business systems can appear intimidating to the small business owner. However, business systems can be as easy as creating written checklists of how you do things. Go back to chapter 9 to identify what you need to focus on to create great systems for your business.

13. TEMPTED TO TRY TO DO EVERYTHING YOURSELF

One of the biggest mistakes you can make is to believe that you can become a "self-made" man or woman. As chapter 10 says, the bigger the dream, the better the team needed. Identify and assemble the internal and external teams that you will need to create a small business and a big life.

14. TEMPTED TO BE OVERLY OPTIMISTIC WHEN YOU ARE JUST STARTING OUT

Avoid being overly optimistic, believing you will be profitable from the very first day and projecting very big profits for your first year. One of the main reasons for failure for small business owners is running out of money. Being overly optimistic will blind you to the reality of what is required to be a success. Build your business from a realistic foundation by creating an accurate budget for your first three years of business. You can go to the Small Business Administration website, www.sba.gov, to discover expected expenses for your type of small business.

15. TEMPTED TO BUY THE BEST EQUIPMENT AND HIRE MORE PEOPLE THAN YOU NEED

You need to hire or buy the necessary equipment required to run your business efficiently and effectively. I did not say that you had to buy the most *expensive* equipment—just what you need to create the product or service to keep your clients coming back. Start by creating a budget of the expected expenses for your type of small business. Go to the Small Business Administration Web site for help. Also, you need to invest not necessarily in more people, but in the best people you can find. There is a saying in Spanish, *Lo barato sale caro*, meaning you get what you pay for. You're far better off paying for one great bookkeeper/accountant than a bookkeeper and an accountant who are less capable.

16. TEMPTED TO START A BUSINESS WITHOUT DETERMINING YOUR PASSION AND FOCUSING ON IDEAS BASED SOLELY ON PROFIT/GREED INSTEAD

You will never ever have a small business, big life without focusing on your passions. As soon as I hear people ask me what business will make them the greatest amount of money, I start to worry. For a business to succeed, you must be in it for the long term, and that requires passion. There was a wonderful book that was written years ago, whose title *Do What You Love, The Money Will Follow,* is some of the greatest advice you could take.

17. TEMPTED TO QUIT TOO EARLY

All great inspirational success stories are about people going after their dreams and not giving up until they turn those dreams into reality. Their stories are inspirational because these people had to overcome insurmountable odds. All of them could have quit and probably had great reasons to stop chasing their dreams. But what turns ordinary people into heroes is perseverance in the face of challenges. That is also why you need to start a business that reflects your passions. (See temptation number 16.)

18. TEMPTED TO SEEK OUT PEOPLE WHO WILL TELL YOU WHAT YOU WANT TO HEAR, INSTEAD OF THE TRUTH

Remember the *American Idol* syndrome? Don't go to your mom or your employees to ask how you are doing. I have found that you will rarely if ever get any constructive criticism. There are very few Simon Cowells in real life. If you really want to grow your business, you need to bring in outside consultants to help you.

19. TEMPTED NOT TO SPEND MONEY ON YOURSELF AND/OR APPROPRIATE COUNSEL

Successful people always have coaches or consultants. This is one of the reasons they achieve success faster than others. In the same way that you want to find the best people to be your employees, you want to find the best professionals to advise you on the different aspects of your business. You also must make yourself the best you can be by investing in yourself and your ongoing education. Courses, books, and a personal or business coach can help you to keep upgrading your skills and knowledge so you can improve your business.

20. TEMPTED TO START A BUSINESS WITHOUT PAINTING THE VISION FOR YOUR EMPLOYEES

All small business owners are leaders, and as leaders they must guide their employees to a brighter future. No one follows a leader who does not know where he or she is going. No one follows a leader who does not have confidence in the future. To lead your employees (and sometimes your customers), you will need to paint your vision of the future so vividly that the people on your staff can almost see and feel themselves there. Reread chapter 7, "Your Vision—The Source of Leadership."

21. TEMPTED TO GIVE YOUR EMPLOYEES MORE RESPONSIBILITIES THAN THEY CAN OR SHOULD HANDLE

The biggest complaint from new small business owners is that they can never find the right people to work for them. But on occasion they do hire someone really good, and he or she becomes the go-to person. The typical small business owner will take this competent person and delegate so many tasks to him or her that the competent person ends up being incompetent. You may never find enough key people, but if you want to avoid burning out a good employee, go back and reread chapter 10.

22. TEMPTED TO START A BUSINESS WITHOUT AN EXIT STRATEGY (OR SUCCESSION PLAN)

If you follow the tools in this book, you will go from being self-employed to owning and running a small business. Remember, however, the purpose of a business is to give you a better life. Businesses build equity and may eventually be worth a lot. Smart business owners have a strategy as to how they will eventually leave the business. Will you sell it, or will you transfer it to a family member or key employee? Smart entrepreneurs start thinking about their exit strategy from the beginning.

The S.A.V.E. Financial Planning System for Small Business Owners: How to Rescue Yourself from Financial Worry!

Personal financial planning for small business owners is a critical step in achieving a successful small business, big life. For many entrepreneurs, starting a small business is a cause of major personal financial hardship. However, you must keep your personal finances separate from the business finances. It's the only way to stay sane and protect your financial future. As a Certified Financial Planner, I work with all my clients to make sure they build a solid personal financial foundation first. To help you prepare financially, I will share with you an outline that I use with my business consulting clients. I could write a book just on the S.A.V.E. concept. Here, I'm presenting an overview of our program to make you aware of what you will need to focus on in your personal finances so you can care for yourself and your family.

S.A.V.E. stands for the four steps to building your personal financial foundation.

SOLID FINANCIAL FOUNDATION
FOR YOUR BUSINESS

1. **Create an emergency cash reserve.** Save as much money as you can to help overcome the shortages in cash flow during the first few months (or even the first couple of years) of your business. Put the money in a liquid cash management account so you can have immediate access to the funds.

2. **Protect yourself with the right insurance.** If you are starting your business on your own without any partners or other financial support, make sure you have the following insurance policies:

   • Health Insurance

   • Life Insurance

   • Disability Insurance

   • Property and Casualty Insurance (including Liability)

   • Workers' Compensation Insurance (if you have employees)

   • Errors and Omissions Insurance (if you are providing certain types of services, such as accounting, tax preparation, etc.)

   Insurance can become fairly expensive if you are not working with an excellent agent. There are many ways to obtain adequate coverage *and* minimize your insurance premiums when you are first starting out. Find an agent who is willing to work with you to provide appropriate insurance at the most reasonable price.

3. **Create a retirement plan.** Please do not make the mistake of neglecting to fund a retirement plan right from the start. The biggest mistake you can make is believing that you don't need to save for retirement because you will make so much money when you sell your business that you don't need to fund your own plan. There are many plans that

require very little in start-up costs. Retirement plans for small business owners include IRAs, Roth IRAs, SEP plans, SIMPLE plans, and single-member 401(k) plans. Check with a qualified financial advisor to choose and set up a plan that's right for you.

4. **Build and protect a great credit rating.** As a business owner you want to know your credit rating (FICO) score, so get copies of your credit reports as soon as you can. This will tell you if you can access many types of business loans. Many of my clients have been given bank loans of up to $50,000 just for having great credit scores. If you find out your credit score is low, you need to concentrate on raising it. Try using one of the great books from Nolo Press (www.nolopress.com) to help you raise your credit score as quickly as possible.

5. **Keep track of personal expenses.** Before you start your business, you need to know your monthly living expenses. Without this knowledge, you may believe that you need a lot less to live on than you actually do. Creating a budget that factors in all your living expenses will allow you to determine how much of a personal emergency reserve you will need to establish. You can get a blank budget form on my Web site for free. Go to www.louisbarajas.com and search in the "Small Business, Big Life" section.

6. **Get tax planning.** Tax planning is not the same as doing your tax returns. Tax returns are mandatory. Tax planning isn't. You will benefit immensely from tax planning, especially during your first two years in business. Find yourself a very good, proactive accountant. Most people think that accountants are good mostly for compliance and regulatory filings, but accountants can do so much more. For many years I worked in the accounting profession, and I know how much a good accountant can help you with your small business. At a minimum, make sure your accountant does tax projections to estimate the federal and state income taxes that you will have to pay on a quarterly basis.

7. **Make a will and create a trust.** This is foundational financial planning for everyone. If you have young children, own property, or have important decisions that must be made in case you pass away or become incapacitated, you need a will, a trust, a durable power of attorney, and an advanced health-care directive. You need to see an attorney who specializes in estate planning. If you have business partners, you also will need a buy-sell agreement. I am not an attorney and cannot give you any legal advice, but I do know that in my years of consulting for business clients, this is the most neglected area of financial planning.

AUTOMATE YOUR INVESTING

I recommend you buy and read David Bach's book, *The Automatic Millionaire.* The core of his message comes down to putting your entire personal financial plan on automatic pilot. Left on our own, we will rarely if ever save. We get inspirational "saving moments," but they are fleeting. Here are some tips for setting your financial foundation on "cruise control."

1. Have your bank automatically withdraw money monthly from your checking account and transfer it into an emergency reserve savings account.

2. Have your insurance company automatically withdraw any insurance premiums from your checking account.

3. Have your payroll company automatically deduct money from your paycheck, or have money automatically withdrawn from your checking account, and transferred into your retirement plan.

4. Buy a personal budget tracking program like Quicken and set yourself up to pay your bills through the Internet. (Your bank can help you with this as well.)

5. Have your accountant or bookkeeper do your income tax projections, create quarterly estimated tax vouchers, and send you a reminder notice when payments are due.

VARIETY IN YOUR INVESTMENTS

When it comes to owning real estate, it's always about location, location, location. When it comes to investing, it's about diversification, diversification, diversification. You need to know where to invest your money for your emergency reserve account, your retirement plan, and other investment goals. For a beginner's guide to investing, please see my book *The Latino Journey to Financial Greatness*. If you are going to hire a financial planner or investment consultant, make sure that he or she is a Certified Financial Planner *and* a Registered Investment Adviser. I said "and," not "or"—ideally they should be both Certified *and* Registered. A Certified Financial Planner has taken courses, been tested, and has received the designation as a CFP® from the CFP Board of Standards. A Registered Investment Adviser is licensed by the state or the Securities & Exchange Commission (SEC). Registered Investment Advisers can make investment decisions for individuals. A stockbroker and/or adviser from your bank can sell you investments and tell you what they recommend, but they aren't allowed to build an investment portfolio for you. With a CFP and a Registered Investment Adviser as your financial adviser, you are more likely to get quality advice on diversifying your investments in the best way for your particular circumstances.

EDUCATE YOURSELF ABOUT MONEY

Education about money means that you need to read good, consumer-friendly information about money. You do not need to become an expert, but you should understand the basics of financial planning. There are a lot of great books on financial planning. Some of them are the *Dummies* books; others are the self-help guides published by Nolo Press. You can find them at any bookstore or online.

However, I don't believe that you can do it alone. I believe that you need an expert financial planner to help you. People who are successful in business focus on strengthening their unique talents, and then they hire the best consultants to advise them on the other parts of creating and running a successful business. Make sure you work with a financial planner who charges for honest and objective advice. Most planners are really salespeople who earn their entire salaries on commission. Don't fall into the trap of believing them when they tell you that their company is paying them. Their commissions come from your investment returns. Look for a fee-based or fee-only Certified Financial Planner and Registered Investment Advisor.

Additional Small Business Resources

GREAT BOOKS TO CONTINUE YOUR READING

Bach, David. *The Automatic Millionaire: A Powerful One-Step Plan to Live and Finish Rich.* New York: Broadway Books, 2003.

————. *Start Late, Finish Rich: A No-Fail Plan for Achieving Financial Freedom at Any Age.* New York: Broadway Books, 2005.

Barajas, Louis. *The Latino Journey to Financial Greatness: The 10 Steps to Creating Wealth, Security, and a Prosperous Future for You and Your Family.* New York: HarperCollins, 2003.

Buckingham, Marcus and Donald O. Clifton. *Now, Discover Your Strengths.* New York: Simon & Schuster, 2001.

Collins, Jim. *Good to Great: Why Some Companies Make the Leap . . . And Others Don't.* New York: HarperCollins, 2001.

Covey, Stephen R. *The 7 Habits of Highly Effective People.* New York: Simon & Schuster, 1990.

Gerber, Michael E. *The E-Myth Revisited: Why Most Small Businesses Don't Work and What to Do About It.* New York: HarperCollins, 1995.

Lencioni, Patrick. *The 5 Dysfunctions of a Team: A Leadership Fable.* San Francisco, CA: Jossey-Bass, 2002.

Maxwell, John C. *The 17 Indisputable Laws of Teamwork: Embrace Them and Empower Your Team.* Nashville, TN: Nelson Business, 2001.

————. *The 21 Irrefutable Laws of Leadership.* Nashville, TN: Nelson Business, 1998.

Sullivan, Dan. *The Laws of Lifetime Growth: Always Make Your Future Bigger Than Your Past.* San Francisco, CA: Berrett-Koehler Publishers, 2006.

GREAT BUSINESS ORGANIZATIONS & WEB SITES
U.S. Small Business Administration (www.sba.gov)
Service Corps of Retired Executives (www.score.org)
U.S. Chamber of Commerce (www.uschamber.com)
Minority Business Development Agency (www.mbda.gov)
U.S. Hispanic Chamber of Commerce (www.ushcc.com)
National Association of Women Business Owners (www.nawbo.org)
National Black Chamber of Commerce (www.nationalbcc.org)

FREE OR LOW-COST BUSINESS COUNSELING
Small Business Administration SBA (www.sba.gov)
Small Business Administration in Spanish (www.sba.gov/espanol)
Small Business Development Centers (www.sba.gov/sbdc)
SCORE Counselors to America's Small Business (www.score.org)
SCORE in Spanish (www.score.org/hispanic.html)
SCORE for Women (www.score.org/women.html)
Minority Business Development Agency (www.mbda.gov)

REGULATORY BODIES
Internal Revenue Service (www.irs.gov)
Internal Revenue Service in Spanish (www.irs.gov/espanol)
Department of Labor (www.dol.gov)
Equal Employment Opportunity Commission (www.eeoc.gov)
Social Security Administration (www.ssa.gov)
Social Security Administration in Spanish (www.ssa.gov/espanol)

Business Resource Organizations

U.S. Chamber of Commerce (www.uschamber.com)

U.S. Hispanic Chamber of Commerce (www.ushcc.com)

National Black Chamber of Commerce (www.nationalbcc.org)

National Association of Women Business Owners (www.nawbo.org)

Society for Human Resource Management (www.shrm.org)

International Association for Human Resource Information
   Management (www.ihrim.org)

To Find a Financial Professional

American Institute of Certified Public Accountants (www.aicpa.org)

Financial Planning Association (www.fpanet.org)

Other Resources

For forms from chapter 6 (creating your life blueprint):
   www.louisbarajas.com

For a budget tracking form (appendix C): www.louisbarajas.com

For a copy of a business blueprint: www.louisbarajas.com

For a business plan template: www.sba.gov

For books on raising your credit score and about basic business
   planning: www.nolopress.com

For a copy of a free credit report: www.annualcreditreport.com

About the Author

uthor, entrepreneur, and Certified Financial Planner Louis Barajas is
an embodiment of the American dream. Born in the East Los Angeles
barrio, the son of Mexican immigrants, at age thirteen Louis started doing
the taxes for his father's ironworking business. He graduated from UCLA in
1984, received his MBA from Claremont Graduate School in 1987, and
attained a Certified Financial Planner designation from the Denver College
of Financial Planning in 1990.

In 1991, after several years' experience at major accounting and financial
firms in Southern California, Louis returned to East Los Angeles to establish
his own financial planning firm, Louis Barajas & Associates. Louis wished to
make a difference with the kind of people he grew up with—hard-working
men and women who, because of lack of information or understanding,
often made bad financial choices that kept them from achieving the success
and security they deserved. Today his financial planning firm, Louis Barajas
Wealth & Business Planning, helps individuals attain their financial goals
through the proper implementation of smart investment and business
strategies.

Louis Barajas has become a nationally recognized expert in financial and business issues for the underserved. His first book, *The Latino Journey to Financial Greatness* (HarperCollins, 2003; published in Spanish in 2004, entitled *El Camino a la Grandeza Financiera*), became a best seller in both languages and was praised by influential Latinos such as Henry Cisneros, Montezuma Esparza, Edward James Olmos, David Lizarraga, Marcos Witt, and Lionel Sosa. In 2005, he was named AOL's Latino small business expert; in addition to answering queries from people all over the world, he conducted live online chat sessions monthly.

Louis was the first Latino to be selected for the National Board of the Financial Planning Association (FPA), a 27,500-member organization that fosters the value of financial planning and advances the financial planning profession. He served on the national board from January 2004 until December 2006. He also served as the board liaison for the Pro Bono and Public Issues Committees of the organization.

Louis' financial expertise has been recognized by many publications and organizations. National companies, including Sears, DaimlerChrysler, Nationwide Insurance, JPMorgan Chase, and Bank of America have endorsed his work. *Mutual Funds Magazine* named him one of the Top 100 Financial Advisors in the United States, and he was recognized as one of the 100 Top Hispanics in Orange County, California. In 2004, he appeared on the cover of *Hispanic Journal*, and he was featured on the cover of the March 2005 issue of *Hispanic Business*. In 2006, *Latin Business Magazine* included Louis in its list of 100 outstanding Hispanics.

From 1997 to 2001, Louis wrote a weekly financial and consumer advocacy column called "Entre Numeros" for the business section of *La Opinion*, the largest Spanish-language newspaper in the United States. He is a contributing writer to many other magazines, newsletters, and Web sites, and has published more than 300 articles. In May 2006, he won the Business Journalist of the Year Award for the Los Angeles Division of the Small Business Administration. Louis is a highly sought after keynote speaker for local, regional, and national conferences. He has been profiled, appeared as a guest, or quoted on more than 1,000 local and national television and radio programs such as CBS *Sunday Morning*, CNBC,

Univision, CNN en Español, ABC NEWS, *Despierta America, El Show de Rocio*, and National Public Radio, and in print media such as the *Los Angeles Times, Hispanic Magazine, Hispanic Business Magazine, Hispanic Journal*, and *Latina Magazine*.

Today Louis conducts seminars and workshops throughout the country to help business owners create systems to help them enjoy more balanced lives. His knowledge product company, Financial Greatness, Inc., provides books, seminars, workshops, and other products to promote financial abundance for individuals and organizations.

Louis Barajas is clearly recognized as the leading national advocate for financial literacy for the working class. His purpose in life is to be the catalyst in helping people of all income levels attain their life goals. In his books, speeches, seminars, and business and personal coaching, he makes the complex and overwhelming world of finances comprehensible as he teaches people at every economic level the simple, practical, and powerful strategies to achieve financial greatness.

To share your personal business stories with Louis Barajas, or to contact him for a workshop or speaking engagement, please e-mail him at louis@louisbarajas.com.